HYPNO-SCRIPTS

Titles by Mary Deal

Fiction
The Ka, a paranormal Egyptian suspense
River Bones, the original Sara Mason Mystery
The Howling Cliffs, 1st sequel to River Bones
Legacy of the Tropics, adventure/suspense
Down to The Needle, a thriller

Collections
Off Center in the Attic – Over the Top Stories

Nonfiction
Write It Right – Tips for Authors – The Big Book
Hypno-Scripts: Life-Changing Techniques Using
Self-Hypnosis and Meditation

HYPNO-SCRIPTS

Life-Changing Techniques Using Self-Hypnosis and Meditation

Mary Deal

ISBN-13: 978-1514824306
ISBN:10-1514824302

Library of Congress Control Number: 2015915019
Mary Deal, Honolulu, Hawaii

CreateSpace Independent Publishing Platform
North Charleston, SC

Honolulu, Hawaii USA

Unending gratitude to two people who, throughout my early life,
guided me in the right direction, my parents:

Helen May Morris
Candido A. Ramirez

CONTENTS

SECTION TWO: MEDITATION

CONCLUSION

CONTRIBUTORS AND THEIR BOOKS

BIBLIOGRAPHY

AUTHOR BIOGRAPHY

Introduction
With Disclaimer

Focus concentration within to find your true purpose.

A thin window of consciousness differentiates two states of the mind – self-hypnosis and meditation – and this book explains their similarities and defines each condition and accessibility. If curious enough to at least peruse this book, then the ability to learn these techniques are already a part of your consciousness and soon to be recognized. Lucky you! Your subconscious is prompting you to investigate. It is saying that you are capable of deeper states of mind.

Instruction in this book may help ease the newcomer into a practice of self-hypnosis or meditation through discovering the powers available through the human mind. Those already practicing may find new techniques to enhance what they already know. Techniques presented here were used in private hypnotherapy and meditation sessions and meant to instill deepest trances. They are not meant to be get-in-get-out quickie therapies. This is deep profound hypnosis.

Many people have tried to focus to learn either self-hypnosis or meditation and failed. Applied concentration and knowing what to expect once entranced may be what was missing. Also a hindrance is attitude (*"I know this isn't going to work!"*) and lack of imagination.

The instructions in this book are meant for those wishing to learn and use the techniques of self-hypnosis and/or meditation for self-improvement. Easy yet powerful scripts are provided so you have something to work with while in either state. These examples ground you so that you do not end up asking What next? once you are entranced.

This book is written from my own experiences as a life-long practitioner in both self-hypnosis and meditation, and in more recent years, a counselor as a Certified Clinical Hypnotherapist (now retired).

This book is not meant to replace in-person teaching or therapy sessions with a trusted therapist. Serious situations or problems should be managed through in-person sessions with a doctor, psychologist, or licensed hypnotherapist. Self-hypnosis is exactly what the term implies. It is a person applying hypnosis to him or herself. Self-hypnosis can be learned individually, from a therapist, or in groups, but ultimately, self-hypnosis is practiced alone in private.

Self-hypnosis and meditation are two related states of mind, each intended for different purposes. What good is self-hypnosis? Or how many times have you tried to meditate only to feel nothing happened and that you failed?

Do you wish you had more power over your own mind, to become all that you can be? All good intentioned chants, mantras, prayers, and other positive programming work best when you reach a deeper state of mind. Discover your potential through unleashing the power of your mind. The secret is in accessing these states through easy techniques presented here, in thoroughly explained examples. The few examples provided here are only a minute sampling of what can be accomplished and hopefully stimulate curiosity to see how far you can take your abilities.

This book is not meant to be all-inclusive of information about self-hypnosis or meditation. Hundreds, maybe thousands of books are published and still more topics and approaches to these modalities exist to write about. This book's purpose is to aid you to learn the easy yet necessary techniques to practice, to clear the mind, and set your intention.

For those already practicing, these techniques may offer ways to deepen existing trances to enhance that which you already know. Here, we remain focused on opening that window of consciousness between self-hypnosis and meditation, but along the way, I've added some gems of wisdom and lots of examples of what may be accomplished in either state once you've become proficient in your practice.

The rewards are infinitesimal and go far beyond anything that could be included in this brief treatise to get you started.

Get to know the wonder of the mind, working through the wondrous human brain.

I do not allude to God, Buddha, Krishna, or any deity. The point made here is that we are all connected to a greater consciousness, the *Collective Unconscious*, as Carl Jung explained. We are connected to the all-encompassing Source from which we each draw personal power.

"He who looks outside, dreams;
he who looks within, awakens."

~ Carl Jung

To think that because we are the center of our personal universe and therefore no higher power exists is a fallacy that keeps anyone from achieving their soul's desire.

Whether self-hypnosis or meditation, two reasons exist for failure:

1) Someone warned you that accessing the deeper mind is not possible and that, if successful, you'd be playing with the devil, and,
2) You believed them.

Some say, "I'll never reach that state." Or they say, "Done that already but I lost the ability." Others say, "I don't want to know what's in my mind." They are afraid of finding something horrible with which they cannot face about themselves or wish not to have made known.

Beliefs are the issues that most people face when they do not succeed at accessing personal strengths. Hypnosis can be a powerful tool in opening or re-opening and restoring a natural human ability.

* What made you believe you did not possess these normal human qualities?
* What happened to convince you that you lost the powers you once had?

Hypnosis can take you back to your original point of *disbelief* to remove it and/or to your most successful time when this ability was active and then reactivate it.

A reputable hypnotherapist can regress you to the origin of these self-defeating beliefs, restore self-confidence, and help reactivate the powers of mind that have always been yours, or....

Self-hypnosis can take you into a deep state of mind and open receptivity to all that is good about you that is waiting to be acknowledged; all that is good that you are capable of receiving and expressing in your lifetime.

That doesn't imply that you'll rise from a hypnosis or meditation session and suddenly everything important you wish to change or conquer comes into being. It means you continue to practice your chosen techniques: hypnosis to change beliefs or other issues and habit control; meditation for letting go, allowing all your good to manifest, without dictating what that might be or how it may come to you.

You are the center of your universe – not the center of *the* universe but *your* universe. You have the power to direct and control your life but no one individual is the Ultimate Power. We are all part of a greater consciousness and that larger power, that force, is what becomes activated in us when we practice opening to our highest selves. Practice it, believe in it, and wondrous changes begin taking place within you, in your thinking, your day-to-day life, and your world in general.

Be serious about your practice. Be devoted and not allow anything or anyone to distract you from your daily routine. Your mind begins to eagerly wait for these sessions, too, and acts disappointed when you do not practice.

Your mind is a magnificent instrument that works only for you. Isn't it time to let you be all that you can be?

For anyone who has tried hypnosis or meditation and failed but still maintains a desire to master self-hypnosis techniques, consider seeing a hypnotherapist, maybe just once. Fueled by your desire, as little as one session can take you into a deep trance and instill a **Cue** that you go into self-hypnosis each time you try. Then you can work gleefully on your own from that point on with self-hypnosis.

Nearly all of the information in this book was recorded and sold on individual cassette tapes in the 1990s. You may see similarities in some of the Inductions because each was created individually and not all of my clients bought all of my tapes, so information had to be thorough for each Induction and Script. Too, not everyone reading this book will need every Induction of Script.

I've long heard, "When will you to publish a book?" This book writing is in response to those many requests. All Scripts have been rewritten and vastly improved upon for book format in today's world.

This book is written in two parts. Accessing deeper states of mind can be accomplished with self-hypnosis as well as meditation. Once you are adept at either technique, the distinction between the induction to either state of mind blurs. The window of consciousness that separates the two is wide open. Are you ready?

Hypnosis, whether with a counselor or through self-hypnosis, allows a person to affect changes in thinking and habit patterns. The results can be gradual, in some instances, unexpected and wondrously stunning. Self-hypnosis can also facilitate a meditative state by cueing yourself to relax and clear a cluttered mind before going into meditation.

Meditation accesses deeper states of mind usually for spiritual purposes. The deepest states of meditation allow a person to get past being stuck in the fascination of the occult; not meaning anything against occult studies, simply meaning more exists beyond that realm of experience. Beyond is where our souls yearn to go. Occult and metaphysical studies are but a small step along the pathway toward higher consciousness and Illumination.

Both hypnosis and meditation are mind processes and both are capable of detoxifying and improving one's life and being overall. Once a person is adept at the techniques, it becomes simply a matter of using a cue or mantra to access that deeper state of mind where either purpose can be addressed. How glorious!

Techniques presented here may appeal to those who feel they do not go deep enough into hypnosis or meditation when they must remain conscious to read or talk out loud. I learned naturally to think myself into these processes after committing them in memory and feeling.

Feeling is important because you can also feel your way into a deep state. I never went deeply into hypnosis by remaining conscious and speaking out loud. Yet, I've included a bonus Induction for those wishing to open their eyes and read.

DISCLAIMER: If you are under the treatment of a therapist, have untreated psychological problems, may be pregnant, or have other reasons for caution, then you are required to see a physician or therapist before attempting any of these techniques. In such cases, any hypnosis should be induced by a professional.

Self-hypnosis should not be used for serious physical and psychological problems unless first consulting a physician or therapist.

Self-hypnosis can be used to correct problems of a more serious nature. However, with those cases, the person applying self-hypnosis would have to have a thorough knowledge of the pathology of the problem and a solid grasp of the workings of the mind. Only when a person is thoroughly educated in the problem and possible solutions, and educated in the way hypnosis works, can self-hypnosis be applied after receiving professional consent.

Likewise, these powerful techniques do not work when one is under the influence of uncontrolled drug and alcohol use. The mind should be completely free of stimulants.

In using any of the techniques presented here, you agree that you do so of your own volition and are solely responsible for any outcome.

In using any of the techniques presented here, responsibility for the outcome is solely your own and you hold harmless the author, publisher and all other entities connected with this publication in any way.

Section One
Hypnosis

"There are so many things in human living that we should regard not as traumatic learning but as incomplete learning, unfinished learning."

~ Milton H. Erickson, Founder
American Society for Clinical Hypnosis

Why Hypnosis

Have you had one or more successful hypnotherapy sessions in your past? If so, then you know that hypnosis can be a magnificent life-changing experience.

We are all born with the ability to reach deeper into our minds. Human beings are capable of feats most have not dreamed of, simply because all cultures have long denied such characteristics, perhaps out of fear of power. We know power in the wrong hands causes calamities and corruption, so it's best to leave things alone. Though this is true, we're not talking about that kind of power here. Improvement starts with each of us personally. Changing our lives for the better, accomplishes a small but vital part of elevating the consciousness of humanity. This book deals with personal power to change our personal lives; to eliminate blockages that prevent us from being the total persons we are meant to be.

The human mind is capable of miracles and more and more people are finally opening to that fact. But maybe they aren't miracles at all. They only seem that way because for so long powers of the human mind have been denied.

Eliminating problems from our lives is not the only condition we may solve through hypnosis. Have a clear mind opens the door to inner spiritual peace. What can be accomplished then is amazing. This is further discussed in *Section Two* of this book.

If you wish to change your life, to rid yourself of the tiniest problem to the gravest circumstances, you can find the way through hypnosis.

In this Hypnosis section, techniques are presented for inducing an hypnotic state with scripts being included to establish cues and post-hypnotic suggestions to continue therapeutic results once you are out of hypnosis.

Once you are self-hypnotized, pre-planned cues applied while the mind is in an accepting mode embeds the cue – a word or phrase – that can trigger help when repeated in your daily waking state. It can also be a cue to help achieve a level of hypnosis much quicker.

As shown by some of the descriptions for usage of self-hypnosis throughout this book, it's essential to understand and eliminate the root of a situation in order to solve problems or enhance capabilities. Many problems can be over-ridden and simple instruction given that the mind not produce something new to replace the old habit. The *Opening to Creativity* chapter shows one of my own exciting therapy sessions when a technique was used to resolve a problem without knowing the cause.

While techniques in this book relate to deep hypnosis, if deepest states seem difficult to reach, here is some encouraging information about light hypnosis:

Randal Churchill is Founder and Director of the *Hypnotherapy Training Institute*. (See his Biography and book list in the Contributor's pages.) Below is an excerpt from his book, *Become the Dream: The Transforming Power of Hypnotic Dreamwork.*

"The more you practice hypnosis the deeper you tend to go, but it isn't necessary to reach deep levels to be therapeutic. Excellent results in therapy can be achieved in light and medium states. Practicing hypnotherapists can train many of their clients in self-hypnosis for added benefits. With experience and confidence that a relaxed and open state of hypnosis can be reached, tools are soon developed that an individual can use for a lifetime to access the power of his or her own subconscious mind.

"There are many levels of hypnosis and various subjective states can be experienced at any particular depth. During lighter levels of hypnosis feelings of relaxation and passivity are commonly experienced. Additionally, there may be slightly altered perceptions or physical changes such as eye fluttering or a tingling sensation in the extremities or a light or heavy sensation in some part of the body. Persons who don't get much of a response at first will continue to learn and develop significant skills within a few weeks of practice."

Unintentional Childhood Training

My Early Practices

Fragments of memories take me back as far as my being six months old, but my first memory of any kind of altered state of mind, other than raucous childhood antics, are from two years old or so. One peculiar occurrence carried through my lifetime from childhood where it developed into what it is today.

When old enough and my mother thought we siblings were more than she could handle, (we didn't know it then but we could really test her patience), she would point to a chair and tell us to sit and *"...don't move till I tell you. Don't even blink an eye."* Mom could become agitated because we grew up a rural setting free to express more energy than most, and we usually did.

In the beginning I didn't know what she meant by not blinking an eye. As a toddler I closed my eyes and went to sleep. Yet, when told to sit and calm down, I accepted her words literally and knew I shouldn't blink so closed my eyes to keep from doing so.

With eyes closed and simply calming down, I began to notice movement behind my eyelids! Movement like vague clouds continually moving or pulsating through the absolute darkness. It was like being inside of my head looking out but seeing out from the center of my mind, seeing the insides of my own eye orbits in front of me.

I became fascinated with that white swirling effect in the darkness behind my eyelids. After that, it was easy to sit and *calm down*. Any time I needed to rest, I would do so, voluntarily, and close my eyes to watch that swirling effect. That in itself was hypnotic, though I had any inkling if such a word.

At nap time I would not go to sleep till I had seen that curious phenomena. The same with going to sleep at night. Still, no way existed for me to know what was happening.

It never occurred to me to tell my mother, not that I could describe such an occurrence when I was a toddler. By the time I was old enough to describe anything, the swirling behind closed eyelids seemed so normal I thought it happened to everyone and gave it no more thought. Looking back now, had I told my mother when I was old enough to describe the phenomena, she might have thought one of her children was a wee different from the others.

As we were growing up, Mom gave us Bible lessons. Dad was a foreman for a conglomerate of farming ranches and worked sun up to sun down, seven days a week. Mom didn't drive and we lived way out of town. So before starting our wonderfully free weekends, every Saturday morning, Mom would read passages from the Bible and explain them to us siblings. Something happened to me during that time. The haze I saw with my closed eyes began happening with my eyes open. I would be watching Mom and listening but at times I became aware that my attention had *gone somewhere* in my mind though it later proved I hadn't missed a word Mom spoke. I began to look forward to her teachings, maybe because it was a time those clouds intensified. I was too young to read but always wanted to hold her Bible.

One day Mom asked me to get the Book and get ready for our meeting. When I withdrew it from her nightstand and held it in my hands, something swept over me! It was like a current of air but I felt it inside too. Strange, also, it didn't frighten me. After that, I held her Bible every chance I got. Looking back, I believe this phenomena would have happened with any sacred book or text that would have been used.

Little did I know this effect and the swirling clouds would stay with me lifelong and become one of the most important aspects of my personal growth. Nor did I know that at that age when I began to rely on the phenomena that this was the beginning of self-hypnosis and meditation. Though young, still I persisted, voluntarily looking forward to sitting quietly and waiting for that certain feeling to wash to me. I was fortunate to enjoy what I saw behind closed eyes and that kept it repeating. Had I become afraid, I might have turned it off. Or could I?

Using Inductions and Scripts

The hypnosis chapters of this book are written with introductory information for each type of therapy. In those beginning notes, you learn how the techniques make the scripts differ one from another. You also learn what to expect once you awaken from the session. Following that information, the Script for the specific technique is presented separately.

1) Read through the *Standard Self-Hypnosis Induction with Waking*. This is one induction and awakening you may choose to use with all the scripts. Yet, each Script also has its own wording, purpose and waking technique.

2) Read through the Introductions to each of the examples given to find one that feels right for you. Remember also, that you may change the wording in any of these to suit your needs.

3) Decide what you wish to accomplish or work on therapeutically while in self-hypnosis and then choose the applicable Script. Once having induced self-hypnosis, go right to that script and begin.

4) Anything contained in parenthesis is instruction only and not part of the verbiage you would use during an induction or script.

5) Do not try to use any induction till you know what to expect from self-hypnosis once you induce it. **Before you begin, you need to know how to bring yourself out and this is shown after each script.**

For anyone attempting self-hypnosis for the first time, you may wish to read the Standard Induction and Awakening once or twice a day for a few days to get into the feel of what it's like to be entranced.

The benefit of putting yourself into hypnosis and then coming right back out without giving any post-hypnosis suggestions is a great aid in helping you quiet the mind to relax into the process.

It may be wise to read all the way through this book before attempting self-hypnosis. You'll learn what to expect while in the trance state, how to bring yourself out, and how to include Cues and Post-Hypnotic suggestions. You'll also learn how to create cues and post-hypnotic suggestions that apply only to you.

After you familiarize yourself with these techniques, you find you no longer need to speak the steps verbatim. They simply happen within your mind and the thought process and visualization of it happens smooth and sure.

Often times, once deciding to end a session, opening your eyes and moving about ends hypnosis spontaneously. If lucky enough to have gone extremely deep, you won't be up walking around. Follow the protocols to assure that you always come totally out of the hypnotic state and that any post-hypnotic suggestions are locked in.

Many people make the mistake of impatiently jumping right in and trying to get into hypnosis quickly and are not successful. Many feel they may have been successful but don't know what to do with it once there and simply pooh-pooh the whole idea thereby defeating the effort all together. Then they may not have learned how to bring themselves out of trance. Without coming out of trance, negativity they harbor in their denial may take hold because of still being in hypnosis.

For safety's sake for those unfamiliar with self-hypnosis, please read at least the section on hypnosis all the way through before trying to induce it. Doing so provides a chance to find a favorite induction and method of bringing yourself back to the waking state.

Terminology

Hypnosis: A technique to still the conscious mind activity of the analytical left brain. To protect us, the conscious mind, the left brain, censures all we receive, know, or transmit. Truth is cloaked in order that we may not be hurt by that which we do not understand or are not ready to comprehend or accept. Our conscious mind protects us from ourselves until we are ready to learn. It is the conscious mind we make quiet in order to access hypnosis.

Induction: Method used to facilitate hypnotic trance.

Asleep: You are not going to sleep as in an all-nighter. Your mind understands your intention to go into hypnotic rest. Still, some relax into a regular sleep when the word is used. For those people, simply repeat *deeper and deeper*. While hypnotherapists of old used to include the term *hypnotic sleep*, it's passé now. Nor do you have to say *deeper and deeper into hypnosis*. It's too much. The mind knows your intention. All you need to accomplish, simply, is the altered state that hypnosis brings about. That is a conscious state of going deeper into the mind. Consciously.

Now: This word is frequently used to keep the one under hypnosis grounded in the *present moment* of the situation. You are subconsciously reminded where you are each time you hear the word *now*; either in the scene under hypnosis or back in the room where you began.

Post-Hypnotic Suggestions: Information or cues that you instill in the mind during hypnosis.
These either take effect in or affect your waking state.

The term *post* simply implies something carried out after the session, at a future time, depending on how you word your suggestions. *Self* refers to the suggestions given to yourself while under hypnosis. Self-hypnotic suggestion is how you instill what happens in the post-hypnotic period, after you are out of hypnosis.

Embed or **Embedding:** Planting a Cue or suggestion into the mind in a way that it remains there.

Scripts: The wording or verbiage that you instill in the mind to change habits, learn something new, affecting behavior, etc. Scripts are the vehicles for embedding post-hypnotic suggestions. Use a Script after inducing self-hypnosis.

Cues: Cues are words, phrases, or ideas and concepts that we program ourselves to remember or repeat, replacing negative mind-chatter as we focus only on the positive. Cues are used in our regular daily routines. Special ones are used during hypnosis or meditation.

The strongest cues consist of one-word or two-word phrases. However, some people choose a short phrase like a prayer which is repeated continually.

A cue is a word or phrase that refreshes information in the waking state that was programmed into the mind during hypnosis. Repeating a cue in the waking state reminds the mind to act upon an hypnotic suggestion already embedded in your psyche.

Mantra: A word or phrase repeated over and over to facilitate clearing the mind to bring about the meditative state. A spiritual mantra created while in hypnotic trance but meant for your waking state can be used over and over, like a cue, throughout your day or any time. This keeps the mind focused and off topics best left alone.

When creating a personal cue or mantra, it is something that you never reveal to anyone, including your spouse. It is something that works in your mind alone. When you reveal a mantra unique unto you, you have given away your personal power. A mantra is personal power embedded within you. It is to help you. It helps no one else to know it.

Hypnotherapy: A counseling process using traditional therapeutic methods while in a relaxed state of hypnosis.

At a deep level of relaxation, therapy is not hindered by the censuring, analytical conscious mind. Hypnotherapy is also what you do as you apply self-hypnosis.

Hypnosis gently allows therapist and client access to the deeper inner levels where the root of a given situation is found. When negativity is removed at the subconscious level, and inner knowledge is made right, profound release occurs.

Hypnotherapy is a nurturing process enabling the inner self to heal and finally express outwardly as the total being.

Intuitive Growth: Inner knowledge expresses more freely with an enhanced sense of intuition. Learn to identify and improve your level of intuition. You'll accomplish more as you function from deeper inner levels. Intuition is that wee small voice within that says you should or shouldn't do this or that. Without heeding the warnings, we sometimes find ourselves in disturbing situations. Your inner voice, your intuition or gut instinct, is you protecting you, nothing less.

Creative Awareness: Many people have wished to do something creative. Yet, when they try to create what they imagined, they fail. If you can imagine yourself doing something, and see it happening in your mind; it's already part of you. You can already do it! It's the conscious censuring mind that has put up the blocks stopping you from accomplishing what you wish. It can be a simple block like believing you don't have enough time.

Self-Hypnosis can access those abilities and actually remove the blocks that prevent finally accomplishing what you should do easily.

A good example of release is from my own history. While attending a private college to become licensed as a Clinical Hypnotherapist, we had many chances to look at parts of ourselves that we wished to improve. How can we as therapists treat others if we haven't cleared out some of the nagging dilemmas of our lives?

One of my wishes was to enhance my own creativity because I wanted to help others express their creative gifts. I felt held back somehow in my own creative endeavors. In cases of simpler problems, like enhancing one's creativity, it is not always necessary to get to the root of a problem to eliminate it or make change; though it's always encouraged to get to the root of a problem, otherwise, we could simply be covering or glossing over a problem.

9

In the chapter titled *Opening To Creativity*, you'll read almost verbatim the therapist's suggestions and my responses which broke up the blockage to my creative flow. It was truly amazing. I use this therapy session as an example of the ease with which hypnosis can work.

While under hypnosis, I felt the rush of release. It's my hope that others can know that kind of excitement.

Perhaps the particular symbology used in my therapy may not work for everyone, but you can easily find your own symbology once you have reached a fairly deep level within hypnosis. Then you, too, may know that feeling of exhilaration.

Habit Control: If we look closely at our reasoning for doing or not doing something, we find various levels of self-denial. Many of the reasons behind these modes of thinking involve hidden feelings of unworthiness, fear of failure or success, general low self-esteem, or myriad other issues. Unless effort is made, we habitually respond in the same manner.

Hypnotherapy can bring about an understanding of why we prevent our growth and progress, and how we undermine ourselves. When we eliminate outmoded and unhealthy patterns of behavioral reactions, we are on our way to happier, productive living.

Stress Reduction or Stress Elimination: Most of the stresses and anxieties we experience are not simply produced by particular situations. Instead, they are the result of existing patterns of reactions set up in our sub-conscious mind which we follow diligently. Those patterns can be accessed through hypnotherapy and deleted, replaced, or changed to more positive modes.

Past Regression: Though I did not work with regression into past lives in my practice, regression into the causes of problems and dilemmas can be found right here in present lifetimes.

Theoretically, history repeats itself. When patterns become difficult to change, hypnotherapy can locate their origin through regression. Past regression can access any age or time as well as blanks in our memories. A blank in a person's memory is a caution symbol because the person chooses not to recall that which harmed them. If sensing such a blank in your memory you should seek professional counseling.

You may not wish to learn what traumatic incident your protective mind has hidden from you. For whatever reason, your mind hid that period of time, so you would most likely not be able to access it with self-hypnosis. Self-hypnosis should never be attempted in such cases. Simply allow your mind protect you. If it's a must that you should know what's hidden, seek professional help.

* * *

What follows is a perfect example of regressive therapy, administered by a hypnotherapist, and one of the meaningful uses of hypnosis in general.

This example case is provided by Mike Angley, Colonel, United States Air Force (ret), Senior Supervisory Special Agent, Air Force Office of Special Investigations (ret) where regressive hypnosis (not self-hypnosis) was used to resolve a kidnapping case:

"During my 26-year career as a federal law enforcement officer, I had the opportunity to see hypnosis at work in criminal investigations. Having been trained in hypnosis during my college days, I had an appreciation for what government hypnotists did and the process they used to induce the state in subjects. I saw its effectiveness in criminal investigations where memory recall was key.

"In one particular case, a kidnapping witness was traumatized by her experience so much that she could not recall many details about the abduction. During hypnosis, she was able to relax and remember a partial license plate of the kidnapper's vehicle. It proved to be enough information to identify the vehicle, the suspect and to make a timely apprehension. I admit that I was a skeptic of hypnosis prior to experiences such as these, but having seen it at work and receiving the tangible benefits it provided during investigations, I have become a supporter."

Self-Hypnosis Techniques Explained

Vital Information to Know before Beginning

Some who use hypnosis respond well to using the pronoun "I" when saying the inductions, as in "I am going deeper and deeper." That won't necessarily need to change. But when using the pronoun I in an induction, you may find the part of you needing therapy, from which your mind protects you, may reject the suggestions.

Therefore, mentally step out of the process and become the therapist applying these techniques to the patient—you.

Imagine this IMPORTANT concept: If it's easy for you as the I person to go into hypnosis, then the **I** part of your mind would have been able to resolve issues or effect change without the use of hypnosis by simply consciously determining to do so. If you've had difficulty getting the **I** part of you to obey hypnosis suggestions, step outside the picture and become your own therapist.

The techniques presented in this book encourage avoidance of using the I. When using "I will go deep into hypnosis," your *protective mind* might be clinging to the thought, "Yeah, sure! Haven't you already tried hypnosis and failed?"

Are you starting out fearing failure? When applying a self-hypnosis induction, try using "*You* are going deeper and deeper...."You step away from yourself. You become the therapist. Your mind obeys your own voice or thought.

* * *

A CASE HISTORY: A hearing impaired couple asked for written Scripts because cassettes were of no use to them. The woman had been born with minimal hearing and was taught Sign very early in life. She never learned to speak well but learned to read and write. However, she had already struggled to listen to many of my cassette tapes.

The man lost his hearing from a head injury he suffered in his teens and was taught Sign. He could speak but didn't like to because he couldn't hear himself and wasn't sure if he was, in fact, yelling at his wife so she might hear. They spoke using Sign language through an interpreter.

I began to explain how they could convert the word *"you"* to *"I"* when using the Scripts. They interrupted saying that wasn't necessary, that as they mentally read the inductions they would imagine it was me giving them the suggestions. Amazing! They were easy to work with, willing to try anything. Later I learned they had rewritten one of my Scripts to suit their needs and, between the two, had lost over one hundred pounds of weight.

They were utterly positive in their attitudes. They had learned the mind is a magnificent instrument, able to overcome what may seem to others as insurmountable obstacles.

* * *

To begin hypnosis induction, remember to talk to yourself as if you're the therapist talking to you. An exception to this follows in some inductions where the words say "listening only to the sound of *my* voice." Though you are the one giving the induction, the *my* is you, the therapist, giving your mind the induction. If giving yourself the induction mentally, then you would be concentrating on the voice that speaks in your thoughts. This is made clear in the *Inductions and Scripts* where this verbiage is used.

Some people like a gentle induction. Others respond to a more dominate approach. The gentle approach is more sing-song and soft. A lot of words are spoken when exhaling. The dominate approach is direct, with the attitude of *Let's get on with it!*

While music can be soothing and help to relax, it is incoming stimuli that the mind needs to process. At least while learning self-hypnosis and after relaxing, turn off any music so total concentration is on the induction and script.

As you read, notice how many times the phrase *deeper and deeper* is used. The more you say this, the deeper you go. You want to go deeper into hypnosis with each time you perform a session. I hope utilizing these techniques becomes a regular practice because there is much you can do to help yourself through deeper states of mind.

Any time words and phrases are repeated, it is a ploy to bore the analytical left brain. When giving yourself hypnotic suggestions, speak slowly, even drag a bit. It's another ploy to bore the critical mind. The left brain is the censuring part of consciousness that decides what to allow into your mind and what to keep out for your protection. When it loses interest, it stops paying attention, allowing you to go into hypnosis.

Should you decide to write your own versions of these inductions, any repeated words, and all instruction for that matter, needs to be solely that which applies to entering hypnosis. You may be in a meadow as your relaxed place to begin, but do not call attention to the birds flying around, or squirrels in the park and such, no matter how peaceful that feels. They have nothing to do with entering hypnosis and are only distracting.

TO CLARIFY: You may allude to hearing the calls of birds in flight because this takes the mind away from anything distracting. However, don't see the birds landing at your feet or something like that. Birds in flight far out at the horizon, or imagining looking toward the horizon, provides the mind with a narrow focus, disregarding everything else.

In some of the following scripts, you may notice it's okay allude to the breeze washing over you or the sounds of the waves lapping at the shore. These sounds and visualizations tend to produce relaxed feelings. It's necessary to be discerning what to include when writing new inductions.

Speak slowly through all inductions. In fact, never rush through an induction, a cue, a script, or coming out of hypnosis. Slow and rhythmic is the key. Most self-hypnosis inductions are performed internally. When speaking out loud, you may be too focused on verbalizing and that could keep you from going into hypnosis. Speaking out loud takes effort and keeps you in a state of conscious awareness, and that may be difficult to overcome enough to deeply relax.

When reading inductions and scripts out loud, you may enter hypnosis if you can concentrate on the verbiage to the exclusion of all else. That is, if when reading out loud you are easily distracted by noises or movement around you, then you may not go as deeply as you might when reading silently.

I like to count down from 10 to 1 during the induction and then back up when coming out of hypnosis. Simply, counting backwards provides the suggestion of letting go and a relaxing feeling. Counting upward from 1 to 10 coming out of hypnosis feels like becoming alert again. The same progression applies to examples using the numbers 5 to 1 and 1 to 5 which are included with some Scripts.

When using the 1 to 10 counting method to awaken, one of my instructors always said them in a sing-song way like notes on a musical scale. I don't mean like holding a note in a song. She said them together quickly and her voice was happy. By bunching several numbers of the count together each time, it safely and happily rushes you to return to the waking state. This method is included with some of the Scripts.

You can bring yourself out using a slower method that you can create for yourself counting up from One to Ten separately. You would then need to have suggestions for waking between each number. Suggestions would be taking a breath, moving your arms and legs, feeling happy, and so forth, all positive suggestions that make you feel refreshed, rested and accomplished once you're out of hypnosis. My experience with using the long form awakening with clients was that they knew they were to come out of hypnosis and usually popped out half way through.

The mind interprets words literally. The examples in this book offer help to understand why certain words or suggestions may be included and others not. This should be an aid when writing your own verbiage.

* * *

An unusual reverse technique of counting up and down— and one that shows the versatility of self-hypnosis— is given in the script, *The Attic Trunk – Finding Your Gifts*. You will first be counting **up** from 1 to 5 to climb a ladder to get into hypnosis and into the attic, and from 5 to 1 to come out of hypnosis, back **down** the ladder and into the room where you began.

* * *

Spaces between paragraphs and lines of verbiage may slow you down and are meant to do just that, to keep you progressing in an unhurried way. Hypnosis is not something you rush through. slowing down allows the suggestions to take hold. However, be sure to complete any induction and script all the way through the awakening stage.

The ellipsis you'll see often, three dots like this (...) means to take a breath in or exhale at that point, whichever is comfortable to you. Practice by reading a line or two to learn where you need to inhale and exhale. It comes natural.

This book was first formatted with quotation marks throughout that made the pages look incredibly cluttered and distracting, so I've removed them in the inductions and scripts. The way this book is written, each induction and script is verbiage, plain and simple, and easy to understand as to what is spoken and when.

For the true beginner, you may be aware of the chair that you sit in, or the bed you lie upon, but soon these may no longer be part of your thoughts. Concentration can become so deep as to lose awareness of all else except the suggestions you focus upon. Know, however, you do not become unconscious; you become *super* conscious. When concentration becomes keen, directed, the difference is clear.

The first effort in the beginning once self-hypnosis is induced is to give yourself this suggestion:

Each time you enter hypnosis, you go deeper and deeper... deeper than ever before.

That phrase can be included in the countdown of your favorite induction. What you would be doing is embedding the suggestion or cue that each time you practice inducing self-hypnosis, you go deeper than any previous session. Do this several times till you recognize the hypnotic trance happening or, for maximum benefit, include it every time you induce.

Most important is that while the first effort at self-induction may feel as though it produced no results, you **did** go into hypnosis. You learn how to recognize the trance state. This only happens when you make the effort to induce self-hypnosis on a regular basis.

Each time self-hypnosis is induced it cements the process deeper into the mind. Be firm in your conviction to succeed. I have known quite a few people who tried self-hypnosis and felt they failed. Yet, when I snapped my fingers, or made some simple gesture and told them to go to sleep, they immediately fell over into a deep trance. I had not put them there. They had succeeded but needed someone else to prove it to them.

As you ease into self-hypnosis, if your eyes are open when you begin, you may feel a great desire to close them. It's a sign you are entering a trance state.

Sample Scripts are presented for your use once self-hypnosis is induced. Become familiar and try to memorize the wording in these techniques if you are one of those who goes deeply into trance once you close your eyes.

Having someone like a friend read an induction to you till you are in hypnosis not only means they have to know how to be a therapist, you will have turned your attention over to someone else which is not the intention of self-hypnosis. I DO NOT advise having someone play therapist performing any induction to you. That person is NOT an educated therapist but would be responsible for your well-being and would not understand what goes on inside your mind. Too, their presence may prevent you from reaching even the lightest state of trance.

When considering what kind of induction to use, many people are afraid of water, heights and so forth. If you are a person uncomfortable with certain scenes, using an induction about going to a beach or looking out over a cliffside to relax may not work. For those wishing a setting more personally comfortable, I suggest rewriting the inductions with a setting more conducive to your relaxation.

For example, going to a beach can be changed to going to a meadow. Do not embellish. Keep it simple. Rewrite the scene to meet your needs.

The most straight forward hypnotic induction is presented first. Then later other scenes, like a hammock or beach scene, show workable induction variations. The beach induction happens to be the most popular one my clients chose to use. Being at a beach doesn't mean you'll go into the water. A beach is refreshing, with a feeling of sitting or lying in the soft, warm sand and feeling a gentle breeze. It's both relaxing and comforting.

Preparation for EACH Session

Use this preparation before any induction.

To get comfortable, loosen any binding clothing and remove your shoes and glasses, too, if you've memorized an induction and script.

Find a comfortable position to sit or lie down.

Also, find a suitable place for your hands, so they won't fall off your lap when you relax. You may sit in any chair you wish, and try to keep your spine straight. When laying flat, let your arms be at your sides, not across your body.

When settled in your comfortable position, fix your gaze on a spot on the wall or ceiling a little higher than looking straight out. Begin to concentrate on what it is you wish to accomplish while in hypnosis. Think about all aspects of this situation but remember to stay relaxed and not become excited nor upset. Believe everything is working fine. Believe. The intensity of your concentration benefits the outcome of these techniques. With clear intention, your ability to concentrate may surprise you!

This step is intentionally included in some of the scripts: Take a slow deep breath through your nose. As you exhale through your mouth, visualize or feel stress from various parts of your body floating out when you release the breath, as if that breath is like a vacuum pulling the stress out. Wherever you feel stress take a few more deep breaths and see it flow out on the exhales.

Then continue into your induction.

Inductions, Cues and Scripts
Section

"...hypnosis is not mind control. It's a naturally occurring state of concentration. It's actually a means of enhancing your control over both your mind and your body."

Dr. David Spiegel, Assoc. Chair of Psychiatry
Stanford University School of Medicine

A Standard Hypnosis Induction
and Awakening

Imagine now a private place of deep comfort. It may be in a forest, on a beach, in a meadow, any place where you can deeply relax. It can be an imagined place seen only in your mind. See yourself there settling in.

As I count from 10 to 1, you will go deep asleep.
Take a slow deep breath and hold... then slowly exhale....
Take another slow deep breath and hold... and slowly exhale....
Feel yourself relaxing....
Take another deep breath and hold... then exhale....
You are going deep asleep.
Somewhere between the numbers 4 and 1, you will be deep asleep and going still deeper.
Ten

In this special place you've chosen to relax, look out over the horizon as far as you can see in the distance. Focus on that point.
Every breath that you take, every move that you make, takes you deeper and deeper. You are going deep asleep.
Nine

Take another deep breath and hold... then exhale. Letting go.
Every sound that you hear, every move that you make, every breath that you breathe, takes you deeper and deeper.
Other sounds, other noises, help you go deeper and deeper.
Allow your breathing to find its own rhythm.
Eight

As you relax, your eye lids begin to feel heavy, ver-r-ry heavy... and they begin to close.

Let them close.

You are going deeper... and deeper... listening to the sound of my voice... taking you deeper and deeper.

Seven

Other sounds, other noises fade into the distance.

Listening only to the sound of my voice.

Taking you deeper and deeper.

Wa-a-a-ay down.

Six

Your arms begin to tingle. They are so-o-o relaxed.

Your neck, shoulders, face relax.

You are so comfortable, so-o-o tranquil, not a care in the world.

Five

As you relax more, your legs begin to feel ver-r-ry heavy.

Feel the muscles and joints relax... letting go... your thigh muscles... knees... your calves... ankles... your feet... completely loose and limp.

You are so comfortable.

You have no desire to move.

Four

You are deep asleep.

And going de-e-eper and de-e-eper. Wa-a-a-ay down.

Every muscle... every nerve... every cell of your body... going de-e-eper and de-e-eper.

You are so-o-o relaxed and going deeper and deeper.

Three

You are deep asleep and going still deeper, so-o-o comfortable.

Every muscle, every nerve, every cell of your body... loose and limp... loose and limp.

So relaxed, and so at peace.

Two

As you continue to hear on the sound of my voice, it takes you still deeper.

You are deep asleep and going still deeper.

You are very, very deep... and going still deeper... deeper than you've ever been before.

Not a care... in the world... as you go deeper.

One

(Waking From Hypnosis)

Now as I count from One to Ten, you begin to stir from deep contemplation.

One, Two, Three.

As you think about leaving your comfortable place, your attention drifts back into the room.

Four, Five, Six.

You begin to stir, becoming aware of your body once again.

Seven, Eight, Nine.

Become aware of how wonderful you feel knowing you now have a positive way to change your life.

Ten.

Wide awake! Fully alert! You are fully alert!

Bonus: Opening Your Eyes

An induction for opening your eyes while under hypnosis is a must. While these instructions want you to play the therapist giving yourself instructions, it is possible for you to open your eyes while in the hypnotic state. Reading the scripts to yourself is as if a therapist is instructing you.

When you go into this hypnotic session, have your book or electronic reader with you. You may hold them but till total relaxation is accomplished, be able to lay them on your lap or nearby table.

With hypnosis established, you may open your eyes and move around a bit, perhaps to turn pages either on your eReader or pages of a book. I do not suggest you attempt to move around much more than that until you are totally familiar with being in hypnosis, otherwise you may inadvertently pop out. Then any instruction from the Scripts may not take hold. Once you are relaxed, you may not wish at move anyway because the relaxation is so complete. Stay focused on the hypnosis and what you wish to accomplish through the scripts.

What follows is similar to the *Standard Hypnosis Induction* but with variation giving you Cues so you'll be able to open your eyes and remain in hypnosis. When you are told to open your eyes and read, read the Script and the *Waking from Hypnosis* at the end.

Bonus:
Opening Your Eyes Script

Imagine now the place where you sit as being the best place for you to be at this moment, a private place of deep comfort. Feel yourself settling into soft pillows and cushions that surround you, cradling you.

Beside you is an open window with fresh gentle breezes and an expansive view over the area. You have reading material with you. Feel it in your hands. Lay it gently on your lap or on the table beside you.

> As I count from 10 to 1, you will go deep asleep.
> Take a slow deep breath and hold... then slowly exhale....
> Take another slow deep breath and hold... and slowly exhale....
> Feel yourself relaxing....
> Take another deep breath and hold...
> Then exhale....
> You are going deep asleep and receive a Cue to open your eyes.
> Somewhere between the numbers 4 and 1, you will be deep asleep and going still deeper.
> **Ten**

> In this relaxing place you've chosen by a window, look out over the horizon as far as you can see in the distance.
> Focus on that point, concentrating how far you can see.
> Every breath that you take, every move that you make, takes you deeper and deeper. You are going deep asleep.
> **Nine**

Take another deep breath and hold... then exhale. Letting go.

Every sound that you hear, every move that you make, every breath that you breathe, takes you deeper and deeper.

Other sounds, other noises, help you go deeper and deeper.

Your breathing settles into its own rhythm.

Eight

As you relax, your eye lids begin to feel heavy, ver-r-ry heavy and they begin to close.

Let them close.

You are going deeper... and deeper... listening to the sound of my voice... taking you deeper and deeper.

Not a care in the world. You have no desire to more.

Seven

Other sounds, other noises fade into the distance.

Listening only to the sound of my voice.

Taking you deeper and deeper.

Six

Your arms begin to tingle. They are so-o-o relaxed.

Your neck, shoulders, face relax.

You are so comfortable, so-o-o tranquil, not a care in the world.

Five

As you relax more, your legs begin to feel ver-r-ry heavy.

Feel the muscles and joints relax... letting go... your feet... your ankles... your calves... knees... thigh muscles... completely loose and limp.

You are so comfortable and will soon open your eyes to read.

Four

You are deep asleep.

And going de-e-eper and de-e-eper.

Deeper than you have ever been.

Every muscle, every nerve, every cell of your body, going deeper and de-e-eper.

You are so-o-o relaxed and going deeper and deeper.

Three

You are deep asleep and going still deeper, so-o-o comfortable.

Every muscle, every nerve, every cell of your body... loose and limp... loose and limp. So relaxed, and so at peace.

Two

As you continue to hear on the sound of my voice, it takes you still deeper.

You are deep asleep and going still deeper.

You are very, very deep... and going still deeper... deeper than you've ever been before.

Not a care... in the world... as you go deeper.

One

Now you remember your reading material. You've come to this place of rest to learn the Cue to opening your eyes to read the materials you brought with you.

Each time you bring reading material with you as you go into hypnosis, that reading material is the Cue that allows you to open your eyes to read.

Become aware of the material your brought into this session. Open your eyes. Do it now. Pick up the material from your lap or retrieve it from the table.

Continue reading the Script you've chosen and read the *Waking from Hypnosis* at the end.

Learning Self-Hypnosis
in a Hammock

In the induction, cue and script which follows, a cue is planted to cement your ability to get into hypnosis. An alternate method of coming out of hypnosis is also given.

In addition to the repetitive use of *deeper and deeper*, notice how many times the word *now* appears in these inductions. The frequent use of *now* helps you to stay grounded in whatever reality you're in at the moment. It keeps your mind focused on the present whether you're in hypnosis or in the waking state. It's like a jump off place beginning with grounding you in a place to start hypnosis. It's a way to recognize where you are in hypnosis to keep you there while you instill cues or post-hypnotic suggestions. When you begin to return from self-hypnosis, it is the now that grounds you in the waking state once you are out of hypnosis.

This is another induction when you are acting out the position of the therapist when using phrases like "...listening only the sound of *my* voice...." as discussed in *Self-Hypnosis Techniques Explained.*

Learning Self-Hypnosis in a Hammock: Induction Script and Cue

Imagine, now, you're at your favorite resort or one you've dreamed of visiting. You're lying in a hammock at the tree line beside a dry white sand beach. Remember a pleasant time when the weather was not too hot or too cool. It's like that here... with the sun sometimes breaking through the canopy of leaves.

Remember the smells of the salty ocean air... the sound of the surf gently rolling in... and out.... Remember what it was like to look out over the horizon as far as you could see in the distance.

As you begin to settle into the clean soft fabric of your hammock, notice it is comfortably warmed by the sun and forms around your body, cradling you, gently supporting you. Become aware of the sun's warmth, as it begins to penetrate your muscles... loosening them... relaxing them. And every once in a while, a cool, soothing breeze passes over you as your hammock sways... so gently.

You watch the clouds in the sky move slowly... toward... the horizon.... Down the beach... you hear the surf against the sand... in the distance... the calls of birds in flight....

You've come to this place of solitude... and today... as you rest... and rejuvenate... your mind is clear to concentrate on learning *Self-Hypnosis*.

Now take another slo-o-ow deep breath... then slo-owly exhale.... Continue breathing slowly... and relaxing... into the comfort... of your soft... swaying... hammock. Other sounds, other noises fade away as you go deeper and deeper.

Ten

As you concentrate on listening to the sound of my voice, your body begins to relax.

Every breath that you take... every move that you make... takes you deeper and deeper.

Nine

Take another slow deep breath.... Exhale... slo-o-owly... as you begin to feel drowsy... watching the clouds become smaller and smaller in the distance.

Eight

You are going deeper... and deeper. Listening to the sound of my voice... taking you deeper and deeper to learn *Self-Hypnosis*.

Seven

You are so relaxed... floating, there above the sand... as another gentle breeze passes over you... de-e-eper and de-e-eper... cradled in your soft comfortable hammock.

Six

Your legs feel heavy now, ver-r-ry heavy... Feel the muscles and joints relax... letting go....

Your feet... ankles... calves, knees, thigh muscles... completely loose and limp... loose and limp. You are so-o-o at peace.

Five

As you relax further, you arms become so-o heavy....Your neck, shoulders, face relax.

You are so comfortable... warmed by the sun... cradled by the hammock... refreshed by the gentle breeze.

You have no desire to move... not a care... in the world... so comfortable... so secure.

Four

Going de-e-eper and de-e-eper. Every muscle... every nerve... every cell of your body... going de-e-eper and de-e-eper.

You are so-o-o relaxed and going deeper and still deeper.

Three

Now you are deep asleep... so-o-o comfortable as you relax even more... feeling the warmth of the sun... listening to the sea... following the clouds... and gently breathing in the balmy... refreshing... breeze.

Two

Every muscle, every nerve, every cell of your body... loose and limp... loose and limp. You are very, very deep... very deep... and going still deeper... deeper than you've ever been... not a care... in the world... as you go... still deeper.

One

You are deep asleep. As you continue to hear the sound of my voice, it takes you deeper still as you concentrate on learning *Self-Hypnosis*.

(Embedding a Cue)

As you relax... and listen to the sound of my voice... the suggestions I give you take you deeper... and deeper. These same suggestions reinforce your ability to go deeper... into hypnosis... each and every time you practice. And each time you practice... you go deeper than the time before. Progressively deeper... deeper than you've ever been before in your life.

You are motivated to practice regularly. As you feel yourself going deeper... and deeper... into hypnosis... each time you remember the cue or say the words *Self-Hypnosis*... you are aware of the benefits of practicing often. You say the cue, *Self-Hypnosis*, as you begin each session.

With each practice session, it becomes easier... and easier... to slip into *Self-Hypnosis*... easier and easier. Your mind protects you and is in control... as you continue to go deeper and deeper with each session.

You learn how your body reacts or feels each time you practice relaxing into self-hypnosis. You may feel various subtle sensations. You may feel like you're floating. You may feel like you're pulsating. You may feel like you're slowly falling through space. Concentrate on the feelings. Go with it! Your deeper mind knows you are perfectly safe. Go with any feeling as it presents itself. This is Self-Hypnosis.

Gently focus on any feelings, the more they intensify. You may notice it more by mentally encouraging the relaxed feeling, then releasing the thought of it. Feel whatever happens. Go with it. Feel it. Become it.

As you master this step, flow with the feeling that's presented to you. It may vary each time. With regular practice, you'll no longer have to repeat these suggestions. You'll simply sit or lie in preparation for Self-Hypnosis... and the feeling begins. Become it.

Then, give thanks for perfect concentration, and for learning *Self-Hypnosis*, both of which are second nature to you now.

(Waking From Hypnosis)

Now begin to stir from deep contemplation, bringing with you the cue: *Self-Hypnosis... Self-Hypnosis.*
One

As your focus drifts back to where you lay in your hammock beside the beach, you return with a new understanding of *Self-Hypnosis*.
Two

You're becoming more aware of your body once again... knowing each time you hear or say the words *Self-Hypnosis*, it reminds you of the perfectly functioning being you truly are.
Three

Be aware of how wonderfully relaxed you now feel and how easily you master these techniques.
Four

Begin to open your eyes, and realize how wonderfully refreshed you are.

Five

Your attention is now fully back into this room and you are wide awake and fully alert. Wide awake and fully alert!

Through the Gate
Problem Solving

A Word of Caution about this Induction: Major psychological issues cannot be solved with this self-hypnosis technique. What you find when moving through the gate could trigger an abreaction. *Do not use this induction if you are already in therapy or need to be.*

Examples of use would be to find something lost or misplaced. Use it to find an answer whether or not to do something. Use it to remember names or bring back pleasant memories. Use it to find something to help open your creativity. Many uses are available with this induction.

    * Try to memorize or get to know the steps in ways that allow you to visualize and feel each of the suggestions as you progress.

    * Talk yourself through the process slowly. Use this induction with a completely open mind, ready to receive answers without deciding what type of responses you wish provided.

    As you begin to relax for this induction, think about a problem or situation you wish to resolve; only one situation at a time.

    Each time this technique is used, have one problem at a time ready to work on.

    Allow time between each session if you have more than one problem. Plan at least 24 hours between each new situation. It is better if you concentrate on one problem till the results appear, no matter it may take a few sessions to find answers. Then move on to solving a new issue.

Most people have myriad problems for which they need answers. When the mind is programmed to work on one new problem every day for a long period of time, it confuses the mind all the more. The best results are to work on one situation till it's resolved.

When I was led through this script, at the point where I was to peer through the gate, I was looking for an answer to a problem with a hobby, I saw everything from rusted metal car parts to toys. But still, I was told to look for something that could give me an Aha! moment. Keep such a moment in mind as you search for your treasure.

After completing a session using this script, immediately write down all pertinent details of your excursion, no matter what you experienced, no matter what your treasure turned out to be. Write down every detail. If clarity about what you seek didn't happen soon as your gift appeared, then among this written information are the answers to the problem you took into the session.

If at any time, your understanding is not clear, read your notes again. Read them out loud. Hear the message that's available to you.

Notice, too, that as you move through this script, from the moment you walk out of the gate with the treasure and back toward the place where you began, that is the way you are brought out of hypnosis.

Through the Gate
Problem Solving Script

You are deep asleep.

Picture yourself walking inside the edge of a shady forest. You've been here before. It's peaceful and familiar. It's a safe place. It's where you come for solitude, a quiet time alone to think. You're following an inviting pathway.

The branches and leaves rustle with the gentle wind passing high up in the trees. You feel the soft coolness of the breeze on your face and are refreshed. You are truly comfortable in this place you've come to know. You are thankful for the solitude and peace with only the sounds of nature for company.

Following the pathway, you emerge from the shaded light of the forest, arriving at the edge of an expansive meadow, drenched in sunlight, that expands far into the distance. All the tall grass is fresh and new and beckons you to walk through the meadow.

As you walk through the tall green grasses, you notice occasional wildflowers about, in a beautiful array of soft colors, soothing and relaxing to your eyes. The wind gently nudges you onward.

The grasses become shorter, until they form a soft, lush blanket of green across the field. It looks so inviting! You remove your shoes. The bottoms of your feet are cushioned by the padding of deep soft grass beneath every step.

You are so at peace!

You decide to find a place to sit, to think. You scan the field of deep bluish-green grass that expands far into the distance. Then, you catch sight of a small glade, with tall swaying shade trees, and decide to go there. You walk in that direction.

When you find a spot, you sit to rest in the shade of a tall old tree that rustles above you. You are so relaxed... and so at peace! As the shade and breezes refresh, you lie back into the thick soft grass and feel its coolness beneath your body.

This is a perfect place to think about the situation you've brought with you to solve.

You think about your dilemma. Answers come because you've come to this place of peace and quiet, and can now explore a solution.

As you review your dilemma, you remain at rest in the shade, on a cushion of deep, cool grass, with the gentle breeze restoring you. You are so at peace, and totally oblivious to all else.

(Pause only a few seconds)

As your mind begins to drift, you hear the sound of a gate slowly open, then close. The sound gently invites you to look.

You peer around and notice in one direction, there's a high wall. Slowly, a gate begins to open again, and a person walks through bringing out a treasure. The look on the person's face is one of pure joy at having found what they were looking for. You watch that person happily walk away, far into the distance, toward their own meadow.

They have found their answer. You saw by the look on that person's face, the joy they had in finding an answer. Now you know that your answer is nearby. Soon you, too, will know that feeling of joy.

Your curiosity to see what lies beyond the wall is overwhelming. That person found an answer there, perhaps you'll find your answer.

You review your problem. You glance again toward the gate, and notice there's a sign above it. You are drawn to go there. It's irresistible! You rise and move toward the gate.... As you near the sign, to your surprise, one or two words on the sign describe your problem! One or two words describe your problem!

You stare at the sign and read the words. Look closely at them now. See what they say.

What could be on the other side of that wall? Surely, if the person you saw returning found what they needed, you could accomplish the same. After all, the sign has your problem named on it! Now you feel compelled to enter through the gate to find your answers. Your eagerness builds.

Slowly, you slip the latch and begin to swing the gate open. As soon as its open wide enough you peer cautiously through to the other side. What you see astounds you.

Let yourself see what's there without deciding anything about it.

(Pause a few seconds)

You walk through the gate and begin to look closely at everything. You notice fine details as you look for the right answer.

It's peaceful being here. You feel positive and energized knowing now you're going to find the answer you need.

You came here looking for a solution to your problem. Remind yourself of the problem.

(Pause 15 seconds)

Reviewing your problem on this side of the wall brings solutions which vividly come into focus. Resume wandering around, looking at everything. Allow your mind to create wondrous things to perceive. Are there colors? Which colors? What does the area on this side of the wall look like? What was the wall hiding that you couldn't see before?

Again, look around at what you **first saw** as you peered through the gate. What was it?

As you wander around, you'll want to find one thing you can take back with you. Look at everything. It might be an object, anything already in existence. It might be a thought that pops into your mind out of nowhere! It could be something abstract.

Be thorough and keep looking. You'll find something to take back with you, which provides the answer to your dilemma. That treasure is yours to keep.

(Pause 15 seconds and look around.)

Suddenly, there it is! You spot something you know is your treasure, something meant only for you to retrieve.

Pick it up or claim it. Identify it. See it clearly in your mind or feel it in your hands or arms. Examine it. Notice everything about it. It's going to help you solve your problem. It holds a message for you alone.

Joyfully and with your treasure, walk back through the gate.

You hear the gate slowly swing closed behind you as you stand there with your gift, knowing it's yours to keep, and you are deeply at peace.

(Waking From Hypnosis)

Now it's time to return. You walk back through the meadow with its soft grasses and cool breezes toward the edge of the forest from where you began.

As you walk, full realization comes to you. The message of your treasure presents itself in your mind.

(Pause 15 seconds)

You continue walking, returning into the forest and onto the pathway home.

Feel again, the cool breezes against you. Notice how calm, relaxed and refreshed you've become. Think about the message your treasure has provided and know there is still more information to come, an abundance of information your treasure provides to help find answers you need to know.

Returning now.... As you walk your pathway through the trees, become aware... your treasure begins to glow... lighting the way... through the shady forest toward home.

As you arrive home, the way lighted by your treasure, you realize the answers you sought are now yours, in your hands and in your mind.

You now open your eyes. Completely relaxed and wide awake. Completely relaxed, at peace, and wide awake.

Hypnosis at a Beach
Embedding a Cue

This induction is similar to the *Standard Induction* and shows the versatility of what can be changed to accommodate your purpose. The suggestions are re-worded and moved about to suit the purpose of the Script, which instills a Cue, and for the Awakening too.

This specific example is meant to show how to include a Cue into the Induction and how to plant complete information about that cue that triggers each time the cue is repeated, even when not in hypnosis.

At the beginning of the induction and several times during the induction, notice that the cue, *Health and Energy*, is repeated. Under hypnosis you are programming thoughts about the Cue into your subconscious and *repetition* is the key. Then, when you're up and around, going about your day, when you think or say the Cue or hear those words spoken by anyone, you mind is reminded to use the information programmed.

Once you have counted down to the number One and are in an hypnotic trance, give yourself the cue or one that you've created similar to the way it's included here.

Also, the frequent mention of the cue as you're coming out of hypnosis, continually drives the cue deeper into your mind even as you are returning to the waking state.

Hypnosis at a Beach
Induction, Cue and Script

Imagine you're sitting or lying in the dry white sand on a beach. You've come to this place to relax and contemplate *Health and Energy*.

Remember a pleasant time when you were at a beach... when it wasn't too hot or too cool... remember the smells of the ocean...the sound of the surf gently rolling in... and out.... Remember what it was like to look out over the horizon as far as you can see in the distance.

Begin to settle in the dry white sand. Notice that it's comfortably warmed by the sun and forms around your body, cradling you... gently supporting you. And beneath the first layer of sand, the earth is cool and refreshing.

Feel the sun's warmth, as it begins to penetrate your muscles... loosening them... relaxing them.

Then every once in a while, a cool, soothing breeze passes gently over you.

Now you're watching the clouds in the sky move slowly... toward... the horizon.... Down the beach... you hear the surf against the sand... in the distance... the calls of birds in flight....

Take a slo-o-ow deep breath... and slo-owly exhale....

Continue breathing slowly... and relax... into the warm... dry... sand.

As I count from ten to one, your body begins to relax. Every breath that you take... every move that you make... takes you deeper and deeper into *Health and Energy*.

Ten

Take another slow deep breath... exhale... slo-o-owly.... Allow your breathing to find its own rhythm as you begin to feel drowsy. Other sounds, other noises, help you go deeper and deeper.

Nine

You are going deeper... and deeper... watching the clouds become smaller and smaller in the distance... taking you deeper and deeper.

Eight

You are so relaxed... as if floating, there on the sand... as another gentle breeze passes over you... de-e-eper and de-e-eper... cradled by the sand. You are so-o-o tranquil.

Seven

As you slip deeper into relaxation, you arms tingle and become so heavy.... Your neck, shoulders, face relax. You are so comfortable... warmed by the sun... cradled by the sand... refreshed by the gentle breeze.... You have no desire to move... so comfortable... so secure.

Six

Now listening only to the sound of my voice. Your legs feel heavy now, ver-r-ry heavy.... Feel the muscles and joints relax... letting go... thigh muscles... knees, calves... your ankles, feet... completely loose and limp.

Five

Going de-e-eper and de-e-eper. Every muscle... every nerve... every cell of your body... going de-e-eper and de-e-eper. You are so-o-o relaxed and going deeper and deeper into perfect *Health and Energy*.

Four

You are deep asleep... so-o-o comfortable as you relax even more... feeling the warmth of the sun... following the clouds... and gently breathing in the balmy... refreshing... breeze.

Three

Every muscle, every nerve, every cell of your body... loose and limp... loose and limp. You are very, very deep... very deep... and going deeper... deeper than you've ever been before... not a care... in the world... as you go deeper....

Two

As you continue to hear the sound of my voice, it takes you still deeper as you embed the cue for *Health and Energy.*

You are deep asleep and continue going still deeper.

One

(Embedding the Cue)

As you concentrate on *Health and Energy, Health and Energy* are the key words you remember.

You've come here, to this place of solitude... and today... as you rest... and rejuvenate... you contemplate *Health and Energy.*

Your mind and body are the vehicles through which your soul functions on earth. Mind and body work together to maintain perfect health and abundant energy. You're aware of a present inner harmony.

You have many things to do in life, lessons to learn, goals you'll achieve. They all take energy, provided by perfect health. Because of the natural synchronized functioning of your mind and body, you always have perfect health and abundant energy.

Your mind guides you in eating healthy foods. It directs you to drink nourishing fluids. It reminds you to eat and drink at proper times. Your mind directs your body to digest. Then your mind directs your body to use the food and fluids for nourishment, and converts it to energy. It lets you know when to exercise and when to rest.

You have reserves of energy that are never depleted because you follow a nourishing diet. All your abundant energy is available anytime. You may call upon it without notice for a greater share. Your energy is always available in any amount you need. And it sustains you through anything you wish to accomplish.

So with your perfectly functioning mind and body, creating an endless source of energy through perfect health, you are free to function in the world. Your mind and body maintain themselves, each working in harmony with the other.

And so you function in and through them without consciously having to monitor and direct them. Your mind and body, working together, are your greatest allies.

Give thanks for perfect harmony, and for *Health and Energy*, all of which you have an endless share.

(Waking From Hypnosis)

As I count from one to ten, you begin to stir from deep contemplation, bringing with you the words *Health and Energy... Health and Energy*.

One, Two, Three.

As you think about leaving the beach, your attention drifts back into this room, and you return with a new understanding of *Health and Energy*.

Four, Five, Six.

You begin to stir, becoming aware of your body once again... knowing that each time you hear or say the words *Health and Energy*, it reminds you of the perfectly functioning being you truly are.

Seven, Eight, Nine.

Become aware of how wonderful you now feel and how perfectly your mind and body function together. Begin to open your eyes, and realize how wonderfully refreshed you are. Now you are fully alert.

Ten.

Wide awake! Fully alert. You are fully alert!

Radiant Health and Well-Being

The suggestions here show an example of the creativity used when writing and giving yourself suggestions.

Coming out of this session, you do not have to count by using numbers to awaken. You use your own will and intention to come out of hypnosis.

When you wish to return from your starburst, all you need do is ask for a ray of light to carry you back. Expect that ray of light to appear. It always does. It is part of you and always there to serve you.

That's the energy you'll bring back with you. It's never be too strong for you to handle. With time, you'll no longer need to ask for the ray to appear. You carry the qualities of your starburst with you, functioning consciously, easily moving in and out of the deep core of your being.

Practicing this starburst technique is not meant to overlook health issues by not seeing a medical doctor when needed. These suggestions address the power of your psyche. If you need to be treated physically, then you should see your doctor.

Radiant Health and Well-Being Script

You are deep asleep.

As you concentrate on *Radiant Health and Well Being*, *Radiant Health and Well Being* are the key words you remember.

Now... in this deep relaxed state, your attention is focused on *Radiant Health and Well Being*. This extremely deep level in your consciousness is where you find the roots of perfect health.

Accept that your mind is in contact with the perfect health residing within you.

Focus your attention on this fact. Visualize or feel your point of perfect health as a tiny pin point of brilliant light—a starburst high up in your crown—sending cool beams of light in all directions.

Your attention is focused on your starburst to the exclusion of all else. See the brilliance of it, allowing colors to appear if they do, without effort from you. Hear the sound of the starburst radiating as its beams travel outward in all directions. Know that it feels invigorating and so-o-o inviting.

You are irresistibly drawn toward the starburst, toward your state of perfect health. As you draw closer, a great feeling of peace and well-being washes over you. Draw closer now.

(Pause 15 seconds)

You long for the feeling of well-being transmitting from this deep level of your psyche. Draw closer... closer... closer still. Become enveloped by the rays. Draw closer still and float up to the center of this point of light... till you feel its rays beaming out around you and through you.

You are permeated by this core of inner light. It's all you're presently aware of. You are at one with the light, becoming the light, deep within.

Now... at the core of perfect health, notice the many rays beaming rejuvenating light into different parts of your being.

Some rays affect your ethereal body, your over-soul, restoring and maintaining this perfect shell, which transmits messages between your physical self and your spiritual nature or consciousness.

Other rays permeate your psychological nature, positively affecting your thinking, your belief system. Accept that improvements of all kinds are taking place.

Still other rays extend into your physical body, everywhere. Especially to any areas where rejuvenation is needed most.

You are at the core of your starburst. You become the starburst. Gently now, think of one area of your body which would benefit from the rays of your restorative psyche. Think of one area that you wish to return to a perfect state of being.

From your position at the center of the starburst, quickly and easily send rays beaming into the area needing to be restored. Send powerful and sustaining restorative light into the part of you that needs to be brought back to a healthy state of being.

Permeate the area with light.

(Pause 15 to 30 seconds to do this.)

Then send again, strengthening and sustaining a constant flow of restorative rays to this area.

And relax... having total faith that your restorative rays are serving you, quickly, and with perfection.

Now draw your attention back to the core of your starburst. Bask in the perfection you know is there, your own perfection. Feel it. Breathe it into your every cell. Become it. Sink deeper into the center. Sink deeper and deeper into the center.

Know that each and every time you practice this technique, you become the star, bursting with radiant health and well-being. You become your perfection, able to send out strong restorative rays from the depth of your healing center.

So relax now, and welcome the access you have into the level of your psyche where rejuvenation begins. Now that you're familiar with that level of your psyche, each time you come here, you find it easier and easier to do. Each time you visit your starburst, you are able to penetrate deeper and deeper into the center of your point of light.

(Waking From Hypnosis)

Think of coming back now. Ask for a returning ray of light to appear. That beam swiftly yet gently carries you back to your starting point. Come back now.

You easily return with more vitality through radiant health and well-being than you've had in a long, long time.

Now you are back. Open your eyes... wide awake... wide awake and stretch... stretch and feel how you've been rejuvenated.

Now you are fully alert! Wide awake and fully alert!

Allergy Control

Disclaimer: While allergies are in part a medical issue, the instructions here are not meant to replace the help and advice of a medical practitioner. What we seek here is to get to the root of the cause of allergies through the psyche.

Learn these few affirmations so you can mentally repeat them without coming out of hypnosis to read them. Or use the *Opening Your Eyes Induction* and *Waking*.

When using these types of cues, it's understandable to use the personal pronouns *I* and **my**.

Actually naming the condition under hypnosis in this technique has a totally different effect than mentioning it in a mantra, as described in *About Mantras* in the *Meditation* section of this book. The difference in doing so is crucial there and explained.

After repeating the simple phrases the first time, relax and simply tell yourself to go still deeper, then repeat the phrases again.

Once completing any number of repetitions, always remember to use the Awakening. Do not take for granted you can pop right out of a trance state. Do all the steps to give your mind solid structure when dealing with hypnosis.

You can create your own cues for habit control: allergies, nail biting, clearing your throat, increasing creativity, and so on. I would suggest you first learn how the mind translates words literally with regard to assuring you're using workable verbiage. Using the example presented should make it easier for you to create your own affirmations by simply changing the word *allergies* and a fewer other words regarding the desired condition or habit you wish to affect.

Allergy Control
Script

My mind controls the cells in my body.
My mind controls all the cells of my body.
I do not have allergies.
I have never had allergies.
Any sensitivity in my eyes, ears, nose and throat,
moves out through the top of my head, and dissipates now.
I do not have allergies.

My mind controls all the cells of my body.
My mind controls the function of every cell in my body.
I do not have allergies.
I have never had allergies.
My mind controls the function of every cell in my body,
I am healthier than I have ever been.
Any sensitivity in my eyes, ears, nose and throat,
moves out the top of my head and dissipates now.

My mind controls the function of every cell in my eyes, ears, nose
and throat.
I do not have allergies.
I have never had allergies.
I am healthier than I've ever been.
Any sensitivity in my eyes, ears, nose and throat,
moves out the top of my head, and dissipates now.
My mind does not replace allergies with new symptoms.
I am free of symptoms forever!
I am allergy free forever!

(Waking From Hypnosis)

Now, as I count from One to Ten, you begin to stir from deep contemplation.
One, Two, Three.

As you think about how relaxed and healthy you feel, your attention drifts back into this room.
Four, Five, Six.

You begin to stir, becoming aware of your body once again, stretching, breathing deeply and feeling renewed.
Seven, Eight, Nine.

Become aware of how wonderful you feel knowing you have a new method of help to improve your life.
Ten.

Wide awake! Fully alert! You are fully alert!

Tinnitus Reassignment

Disclaimer: Tinnitus (pronounced *tin-ny-tus*) has many causes. It's mostly equated with loud noises damaging the hearing organs and nerves. However, it can be caused by something as minor as emotional stress and as severe as brain lesions among other brain related issues. Temporomandibular joint dysfunction (TMJ) can also cause hearing impairment and tinnitus. So can sinus and fluid levels. Serious hearing problems must be diagnosed and treated by a physician. Those suffering from Tinnitus should see a professional to first rule out any of these and myriad other causes.

I've included this Tinnitus Script in the book because our world has become a noisy place and multitudes of people suffer from this annoying condition. It can delay or disrupt a person from achieving a deep state of meditation, which is another purpose of this book. If you've learned no physical ailment or disease causes your tinnitus other than that your brain impulses are reproducing sound, then the Script which follows may diminish or end the sounds of tinnitus.
   You should also stop believing that you have to learn to live with the condition.
   Tinnitus is the nerves of the brain replaying sounds you have heard. It may have been a blast horn on a fire truck, maybe a police siren, or someone screaming. What about loud, loud annoying music intruding into you private space? Maybe it was target shooting without remembering or knowing you should use noise cancelling head gear. Chances are, if you can't pin point a single incident that started your tinnitus, you won't know which sounds caused your tinnitus because tinnitus does not copy the original sound exactly. Truth is, start with the problem of knowing you have tinnitus. and begin your therapy from that point.

It's not necessary to know exactly what started your tinnitus, but a good hypnotherapist can regress you to find the cause. Still, that is not necessary at all. You can break the loop of the replaying and replaying without know the exact causal sound.

Tinnitus produces intrusive sounds as squeals, knocking, buzzing, or a high-pitched hum in a continuous loop that play and replay and replay. Many people hear more than one sound at one time, me for one. Some sufferers hear noises in the background and choose to live with the problem by simply not dwelling on them. Focusing the mind elsewhere and not dwelling on the sounds works for some sufferers who can keep their minds busy all the time. What about those who wish to stop the mind-chatter, perhaps just to sleep well, or to tune out and get into the stillness of meditation? Why live with the annoying sounds when help exists?

Now all that noise may be diminished or eliminated, depending on how deeply you take yourself into hypnosis. The effort it takes the brain to reproduce these sounds can be reassigned so that the nerve center producing tinnitus has a new job, never to return to tinnitus production. Take yourself as deeply into hypnosis as you've ever been. In a state of profound hypnosis is where this reprogramming takes hold. For most people, it's first a matter of getting deep enough into hypnosis, but again, never stop your induction to try to ascertain how deeply you've gone. Simply set your mind to go *deeper than you've ever been before.*

Some may have instant results. Others may need to practice this Script several times as they notice the sounds subsiding. Whatever happens, don't give up. You'll be retraining your mind.

A Cue has also been added in the Script for you to use in the waking state. The more you use it, the more you affect benefits.

NOTE: I was once rear-ended in a car accident. As a result, I have permanent TMJ problems. Simply put, my jaws sometimes become unhinged. Sometimes they pinch nerves. Coming unhinged is laughable but goes unnoticed by anyone other than myself and how this hurts in my ears. I've had a bit of tinnitus through the years since then but don't know if it started with the injury.

All I know is that over time I began having a huge dislike of loud noises and my tinnitus problem worsened. I was one of those who said the tinnitus was mild enough in the background, but that all changed.

If I worked out too strenuously at the gym, or generally did any strong movements while using the machines affecting my jaws or my bite, my TMJ flared up. During those times, my tinnitus became loud enough and constant and I wanted to scream. No cure or way to correct my TMJ problem exists. I've exhausted all options.

When I'm having TMJ problems, and if my tinnitus acts up, I control it or remove it with hypnosis. Because of my positive reaction to tinnitus therapy while in hypnosis, I believe others may control or eliminate their tinnitus, too, and they don't have to have TMJ.

While researching to find relief, I learned about a recently discovered factor, that the *negative emotional response* to a noise is what causes the brain to choose which sounds to convert to tinnitus. A *negative emotional connection*.

When a sound bothers you, instead of reacting in a disturbed way with negative thoughts—*There go those blasted fire trucks again!*—and negative emotions, immediately change your reaction to a positive one.

One Example: If the blast horn of a fire truck grates on your nerves, that's a negative reaction. What you need to do is **think** that someone in dire trouble will be getting the help they so desperately need. Allow the blast horns and let them go. Cover your ears if you must. Wish the responders to remain safe as they speed away. Mentally tell the people who need help that help is on the way. That's positive. Simply change your *emotional connection* to any sound. In your day-to-day thinking, notice when you have negative thoughts, particularly about sounds. It would be wise to catch those early in your effort to remove tinnitus. Have positive thoughts about sounds when you begin the *Tinnitus Reassignment Script*.

What follows in the *Tinnitus Reassignment Script* is how I manage my tinnitus problem. Understand, however, that I add perhaps another half hour to my session while in hypnosis (not included here), working on both my tinnitus and healing my TMJ problem together. Knowing how debilitating loud tinnitus can be, other sufferers need to have this wonderful procedure. You have help. It starts right here. If in the course of using this Script you find rapport with one set of phrases more than another, it's perfectly fine to stop and repeat that part, any part, as many times as you wish.

Repetition will drive the suggestions deep into your mind. However, do not forget to go through the rest of the Script to embed the suggestions and the Cue into your psyche and to bring yourself out of hypnosis.

Tinnitus Reassignment Script

You are deep asleep.

Imagine that the universe, the Collective Unconscious, contains healing power that you need.

Begin to visualize a pure white cloud floating above you. In that cloud is the cleansing power you need to free you from the effects of tinnitus.

Repeating the cue, *Free and Clear*, embeds this phrase in your mind and has the same effect in or out of the hypnosis, whether spoken in thought or out loud.

Now allow that white cloud to draw close. Thankfully, open your crown like a funnel to receive it as this pure white power source pours into your head.

It permeates your brain, filling every muscle, every nerve, every cell with clearing and rejuvenation. It fills the cavities and parts of your face, clearing and restoring anything it touches.

This restoring flow neutralizes any negativity may be feeling at this moment.

(Pause 15 seconds to visualize this.)

Now, this white cloud flows into your ears. It also comes from outside your body and pours into both ears.

It comes from inside your head and fills your inner ears. Visualize this restorative white flow routing around in your outer ear and inner ear, permeating every cell, every nerve, and giving you clear hearing, *Free and Clear* hearing.
Free and clear hearing.

All sounds enter through your ears and are channeled into your memory banks. Your mind determines what sounds to keep and which ones to forget.
All sound is stored only in your memory banks.
However you perceive it, imagine the channels from both ears, like nerves, flowing into your memory banks, depositing thoughts and sounds, then letting go, to return to collect new sounds and thoughts. Imagine it now as you go deeper.

(Pause 15 seconds.)

Now, without becoming emotional, imagine how you feel when you're irritated by external everyday sounds.
Imagine those tinnitus sounds, however you perceive them in your mind. Imagine finding the nerves connected with those sounds.
Then imagine those nerves leading from deep inside your ears forming a loop, picking up those sounds, and then replaying them over and over and over. See them!

(Pause a few seconds.)

In order to neutralize the negative emotion you feel toward those sounds, allow that white cloud now inside your head to coat those tinnitus loops, cleaning them, scouring them, and turning them white.
Pure cleansing white, removing all traces of sounds replaying.
Removing all traces of negative reactions to those sounds.
Removing all traces of past tinnitus recordings.

(Pause a few seconds to visualize the cleansing.)

Again, visualize your negative reactions to sound.
See the tinnitus loops.
Coat them thick with cleansing white Light.

Clean them of all memory, ready to start fresh.

Cleaning them breaks the connection between the original sounds and the loops.

Do that again. Cleanse those loops of all tinnitus memories by scouring them with white Light.

Cleanse those loops of all negative emotion connected with those sounds.

(Pause 15 seconds.)

The tinnitus nerves have stopped reproducing sounds!
The connection between hearing and tinnitus is broken!
Tinnitus is no longer a part of your hearing!
Your reaction to sounds is positive.
You now have clear hearing. Now!
Your hearing is *Free and Clear*. Forever!

(Pause 15 seconds.)

Now it is time to redirect the nerves in the loop and put them to use elsewhere.

They have stopped RE-producing sounds.

Starting today, those nerves work with other nerves of your hearing apparatus to move sound into your memory banks.

Once the nerves deposit sound, the nerves disconnect from replaying that sound.

All sound moves to your memory banks where they remain quietly.

You understand all sounds as you hear them and you react in a positive manner to them.

Sounds are no longer reproduced in a loop.

Now that the loop of replaying sounds is broken, your natural hearing becomes perfectly clear.

Rejoice!

You have cleared the loop between original sound and the continuous replaying.

You have reassigned the nerves of the loop to new responsibilities.

All your auditory nerves now transmit sound into your memory banks and then disconnect, ready to pick up new sounds to transmit.

This leaves you with clear hearing and even better memory. *Free and Clear*. Now!

Visualize the process of redirecting those cleansed nerves to work the same as all auditory nerves, depositing new sounds into your memory banks and then disconnecting. See it now as you go deeper.

(Pause 30 seconds)

Now, with all sounds being stored quietly in your memory banks, once again visualize the white cloud filling your ears.

The cleansing white cloud permeates all parts of your outer and inner ears. Every muscle, every cell, every nerve.

Clear hearing is restored as the white cloud withdraws, ready to return when called upon. Your hearing is now *Free and Clear*. Forever!

(Pause 30 seconds
to allow these suggestions to embed.)

(Waking From Hypnosis)

Now, as I count from One to Ten, you begin to stir from deep contemplation bring with you the cue, *Free and Clear.*
One, Two, Three.

As you think about how relaxed and healthy you feel, your attention drifts back into this room with the words *Free and Clear*.
Four, Five, Six.

You begin to stir, becoming aware of your body once again, stretching, breathing deeply, and feeling renewed.
Seven, Eight, Nine.

Become aware of how wonderful you feel knowing you have a new method of help to improve your life. Your hearing is now *Free and Clear*.
Ten.

Wide awake! Fully alert! You are fully alert!

Rest and Relaxation

Some people simply can't relax. After busy days time should be taken to rest and rejuvenate both the mind and body. The techniques here are positive suggestions to practice in or out of hypnosis. However, learning them while under hypnosis assures the suggestions are restoring your natural ability to rest and relax when necessary.

For this session, again, you'll easily memorize the instruction in the Script. Once having instilled this technique while under deep hypnosis, be assured, trying it while not under hypnosis has the same deep relaxing effect.

If at any time you cannot visualize a silky flawless cloud of radiant **pure** white, stop and do not proceed till you can see a cloud that is clear. What you visualize must be pure and clean.

When younger and I would stay out late and feel tired at work the next day, I would use this technique quietly at my desk to power me through the work day.

Once established, this technique works as deeply for five minutes of rest as it does for thirty minutes, or an hour or for a deep restful sleep at night. Day sleepers who find it difficult to sleep or get to sleep benefit from this technique. Should you wake in the middle of sleep, you can use this technique to relax you back into slumber.

Anytime you need from a few minutes of rest to an entire night of tranquility, this technique provides the ability to cast away anything that stands between you and total relaxation.

Rest and Relaxation Script

You are deep asleep.

Feel your body in its totally relaxed state. Your body is heavy and limp and you are completely at peace.

A brilliant cloud of pure white forms above your head. It's connected far out in space and time and hovering above you, waiting to help restore you.

The silky cloud draws close to the top of your head... and begins pouring into your crown... moving slowly through your brain, your face.... It keeps flowing as it enters the top of your spine and sinks lower still, down into your throat and neck.

The cloud pours into your torso... down your shoulders and arms, into your elbows, hands and out your fingertips. Down your spine, filling your chest and then your lower abdomen and hips, filling your entire torso as it progresses. Still it keeps flowing... down into your thighs, knees, calves, ankles and feet... leaving through the soles of your feet.

As you visualize this force flowing through you in a never ending stream, give in to it. See and feel its powerful current as it sweeps all tension from you. Watch this stream of light and feel it moving through you.

(Pause 15 seconds)

Now check with your body. Does any stress or tension remain, in either your body or mind? If finding any discomfort, visualize dumping these stresses into the current as if flows, which sweeps it away, either out through your hands or through the bottoms of your feet.

Get to know the feeling of this current coursing through you. Check various parts of your body and see and feel the current moving through them. It swiftly carries away all stress and tension.

Then, the flow slows down and settles within your body, restoring and building reserves of energy for use whenever needed. Visualize this pure power within all parts of your body. Feel it. See yourself aglow with this energy. As you become accustomed to the feel of the white cloud, you may seem to float or feel like you're rocking gently back and forth. Allow it to happen. Go with the feeling.

(Pause 15 to 30 seconds
visualizing this current working its magic!)

Give thanks for *Rest and Relaxation*, and for the abundance of healthy energy this technique creates in you.

(Waking from Hypnosis)

Now count from one to five, begin to stir from deep contemplation, noticing again, the deeply relaxed state of your arms and legs. Your body is completely at ease, created by *Rest and Relaxation... Rest and Relaxation.*
One

As you think about how restored you feel, your attention drifts back to the present, and you return with the knowledge of a powerful technique for *Rest and Relaxation.*
Two

You begin to stir, becoming more aware of your body... knowing that each time you hear or say the words *Rest and Relaxation*, it reminds you of the perfectly functioning being you truly are.
Three

Become aware of how wonderful you now feel and know you've learned a technique that not only provides *Rest and Relaxation*, but also an endless source of energy.

Four

Begin to open your eyes, feeling wonderfully refreshed. Now you are wide awake and fully alert.

Five

Eyes open. Wide awake and fully alert. You are fully alert!

Immediate Stress Reduction

Dr. Andrew W. Weil, American medical doctor, teacher, and best-selling author on holistic health, says on an Internet post:

"People who are stressed or anxious are actually chronically under-breathing, because stressed people breathe shortly and shallowly, and often even unconsciously hold their breath. By extending your inhale to a count of four, you are forcing yourself to take in more oxygen, allowing the oxygen to affect your bloodstream by holding your breath for seven seconds, and then emitting carbon dioxide from your lungs by exhaling steadily for eight seconds. The technique will effectively slow your heart rate and increase oxygen in your bloodstream, and may even make you feel slightly lightheaded which contributes to the mild sedative-like effect. It will instantly relax your heart, mind, and overall central nervous system because you are controlling the breath versus continuing to breathe short, shallow gasps of air."

* * *

What would it feel like if, when feeling stressful, a comfortable soothing wave of balmy air washed over you and completely carried away your tension?

Imagine it happening. Do you think you'll feel it? Most certainly, you will! And you would breathe deeply feeling the relief. Breathing deeply relieves stress and is also why instruction tells you to take a few deep rhythmic breaths before entering hypnosis.

Breathing is looked upon as a nutrient the human body cannot live without.

When we feel tense, breathing may become shallow. Shallow or improper breathing is sometimes the cause of people fainting when tense or in shock. That's a time we need to breath deeper. Oxygenating the blood is critical for relaxation, so always remember to breathe deeply.

To relax, whether standing, sitting, or lying, after embedding the technique for dealing with acute stress (perhaps along with the Cue from the Bonus section below), you can perform these techniques quickly without being entranced. Always remember to take a deep breath or two even when not in hypnosis.

Success depends on how deeply you concentrate while performing this technique in or out of hypnosis.

Once this technique becomes established, quickly and smoothly, allow the refreshing breeze to flow over you, from head to foot, right where you sit or stand though you are not under hypnosis. Breathe. As you do this, allow the wave to wash away any tenseness or resistance you feel in your body. You can focus on a particular area you identify as bothered by this stress. You can perform this simple technique repetitively till you feel better, depending on how much time your situation allows.

Use this method anytime you have a few spare moments and a private place to relax. You can do this sitting at your desk at work or sitting in your car when parked (never when driving), and the wave can be repeated in rapid succession to give you a rush of cleansing.

This *Immediate Stress Reduction* technique is for dealing with stress the instant it begins happening, while your stress reaction is being activated and immediately thereafter. You can positively change your stress reactions that creep in unexpectedly while in a tight situation.

Some stresses, occur so quickly we have little or no time to think how we're going to react. Using your Cue, in time, changes your immediate reactions. Till then, when overwhelmed by that all too familiar feeling, there is much you can do.

Any technique for stress that you begin to use should be one that can be performed anytime it's needed.

The more you use your chosen techniques, the more you tell your mind to accept them and adjust to allow them to work for you.

* * *

AN ADDED BONUS: You can instill the following Cue in either or both the *Immediate Stress Reduction* or the *Long Term Stress Elimination Scripts.* The cue here can also be instilled by changing the cue word in the *Self-Hypnosis in a Hammock Induction, Cue and Script* already presented.

1) Under hypnosis, give yourself the cue that in any situation, when you're becoming bottled up, simply move your hand through the air about elbow level, much like you would shoo away a fly. Once or twice is all that would be needed. Believe that your hand dismisses any hint of stress from you. This hand movement is a gesture that's acceptable and mostly overlooked by others.

2) Another powerful gesture is one I used to do and never knew it until someone brought it to my attention.

When I used to feel inundated with decisions to make, people waiting for answers, time constraints and so forth... I would always bring the middle finger of my right hand to my right temple, as if thinking deeply.

Once this was brought to my attention, I tried not doing it during high-pressure situations. I found I remained in a muddled state. It seemed my focus totally left me. Under extreme stress, my nerves gave me goose bumps, my stomach did flip-flops. Other times, I could sense an on-coming headache. Resuming the use of that simple gesture allowed me to concentrate on what I needed to resolve. Touching my temple allowed me to think of nothing else and focus in on a solution to a problem. I would have no stress during or afterwards. I could actually feel on-coming stress leaving my body, as if it simply expanded outward and flew away from me. Having the use of my finger-to-temple being pointed out to me, and seeing how not using it jumbled my thinking, educated me about the value of a simple cue.

* * *

Perhaps you're beginning to realize you could benefit from creating your own cue. Maybe you've thought of a simple gesture you could use. If so, I encourage you, through self-hypnosis, to instill in your cue the power of relaxation and constructive thought.

Many other ways of eliminating stress from our lives can be found in books already written on the subject. Some of those pertain to diet and exercise, laughing, or cleaning up an area around you such as your desk, room or office. A friend who is a good listener can help get rid of stress by allowing you to speak about it. Placing mental emphasis on the fact that you're doing something about stress is beneficial. The point is, do something about it and free yourself. That, in itself, is a positive beginning.

You may use your own cue or one of those I've given. You might use a new simple gesture, perhaps rubbing or tapping two fingers together. Maybe you'll tap your shoe on the floor one or two quick times. Use a technique anytime you wish to work on clearing and improving your reactions.

As you work your cue with a feeling of elation, knowing this tool helps you change to more positive reactions, you are embedding that knowledge in the cue itself. That cue is cementing the knowledge in your mind, over-riding old negative stress reaction programming.

Practice this as many times as necessary. Install your personal Cue with a few simple words as the wave washes over you. The wave washing over you is also a cue in itself. Make use of these tools and see the positive results.

Immediate Stress Reduction Script

You are deep asleep.

Breath in and out with three long deep breaths, followed by letting your breathing return to normal.
As you settle deeper into hypnosis, imagine the wave of fresh air above you. Move the wave down the length of your body from head to toe, smoothly but quickly.

Imagine this wave being completely capable of relaxing you each time you move it down the length of your body. Each time you do this, wherever tenseness appears, dump that tenseness into the wave, however you see this happening, dump the tenseness into the flowing wave. See it immediately carried away from any part of your body.

Do it now. Allow that cleansing wave to flow over you. Dump any stresses into that cleansing current.

(Pause 15 seconds)

Run the wave again, smoothly but quickly.

(Pause 15 seconds)

And once more, smoothly and quickly.

(Pause 15 seconds)

Now, remember the personal Cue you chose to work with for this exercise. In this deeply relaxed state, perform the gesture in your mind and acknowledge that it removes stress. If you have learned to move while under hypnosis, physically perform the gesture. Sense the feeling of elation knowing you're positively changing your reality. Be thankful for it.

In this relaxed, positive state, again execute the cue you've chosen. Do it now **as you visualize stress being swept from you.** Again, say that your cue removes stress.

(Pause 15 seconds)

Do it several times more reminding yourself you're embedding it as a cue that immediately removes stress.

(Pause 15 seconds)

Do it again. When out of hypnosis, rest briefly.

(Waking From Hypnosis)

Now as I count from One to Ten, you begin to stir from deep contemplation.
One, Two, Three.

As you think about your cue and how it eliminates stress immediately, your attention drifts back into this room.
Four, Five, Six.

You begin to stir, becoming aware of your body once again, stretching, breathing deeply, and feeling stress free.
Seven, Eight, Nine.

Become aware of how wonderful you now feel knowing you have a new method to improve your life.
Ten.

Wide awake! Fully alert! You are fully alert!

Long Term Stress Elimination

The slightly varied technique in the *Long Term Stress Elimination Script* serves to take you deeper to remove long-held habitual responses to stressors. We've all responded to difficult situations in habitual negative ways over long periods of time. Those responses can be removed and replaced with more positive action.

Stress can sneak upon us before we know it. That's why it's important to change the overall way we react to the demands of our lives. If nothing is done, our reactions to stress become permanent habits, draining us of our valuable life force.

When we find ourselves in difficult situations, what happens? Stress is not something from outside of us. It comes from inside ourselves. Something in our lives, in our thinking, over a period of time, has helped us program ourselves for stress reactions to various incidents. Perhaps we react the same way our parents or closest friends react. We react to issues in certain ways and, yes, we choose to react in certain ways. Therefore, we create our own stress.

I place emphasis on the word *choose*. If you could choose to react a different way and be stress free, would you do it? The key lies in our attitudes, our perception and our belief system. In these areas, you'll find what triggers your type of reactions to various occurrences.

With these areas in mind, begin to relax expectations of yourself. Here are a couple of examples:

1) It's okay to push to get the job done. But it's not okay to push to the *point of fear* of not getting the job done. Challenge yourself to do as much as you dare, to solve issues and be accomplished, but do not push yourself to the point of fear.

Most of all, don't believe that anything is so important as to have to push yourself that far.

2) It's okay to accept that others may not live up to our expectations. When we realize how human and normal others are, we realize how human and normal we are. All have limitations caused by expecting that which cannot be. It is less stressful to adapt than to push against something we *cannot* change.

Inducing this longer technique works as well sitting in a comfortable chair, but whenever possible, lying down promotes deeper relaxation and that's what we wish to accomplish till you're able to perform the technique without being in hypnosis.

This stress elimination technique goes deeper to root out habitual responses to stressors that we may have used over a lifetime and have inadvertently become deeply engrained. Under deep hypnosis, the benefits are phenomenal.

Right now, breathe in and say or think the words, "Not a care... Then exhale and say "... in the world."

Repeat these small phrases, three, four times as you breathe in, and then out, and let your eyes close. "Not a care... in the world."

You feel yourself relaxing more. The most important thoughts you'll have for the next few minutes begin with, "Not a care... in the world."

Remember that wave of balmy breeze washing over you in the last chapter? For this technique, you can use that same breeze or it can be a slow wave in a gentle ocean. Choose your wave – air or ocean. We're going to perform the wave technique at a slower pace. Get into your comfortable place to relax where you can spend some uninterrupted moments.

Think of a situation that causes mild stress, only one situation each time you perform this technique. Without emotional reaction, get into the feeling of that stress, knowing your mind is now able to release it.

Locate where that stress affects your body. From where in your body do you react most strongly to that one stress? Is it centered in your jaws and cheek muscles as you clench to keep from saying something you'll regret? Is it in your shoulders and neck as you slouch from being insulted? Or is it affecting your stomach? Maybe it's only in your temples. Maybe, your lumbar region? Or your fists.

Take a moment and locate where you think you're affected most by this particular stress you've chosen to wash away.

If you have difficulty locating an area, for this exercise, make your best guess. Simply hold that thought, remembering the slow methodic wave that washes it all away as it passes over and through your body.

In the Script you not only release stress but the verbiage helps you release old programmed reactions to stress. Too, your mind will not replace those removed reactions with some other habit.

You do not need to memorize this technique word for word. In fact, once hypnotized, it's best if you simply apply the beginning phrase – *not a care... in the world* – and then visualize the wave process happening.

Practice this technique under hypnosis till it's ingrained in your mind. This technique is meant to alleviate *reactions to stress carried from a lifetime of past experiences*. It instills calmness and tranquility. It helps override and replace old patterns of reactions.

As you practice this technique more and more, you find yourself reacting to current or immediate stressful situations in a calm, positive, constructive way. As this relaxation becomes ingrained into your reactive responses, you'll find you move through any difficulties swiftly and decisively, without the negativity of stress.

Any single situation that elicits a negative reaction can be the focus of attention as you practice this technique.

Long Term Stress Elimination Script

You are deep asleep.

Imagine a soothing wave coming from above you and moving toward the top of your head. Feel it come in contact with your crown.

You begin to sink farther into your comfortable position.

When the wave reaches the area you believe most affected by this stress, see or feel the stress washed away or *pulled from you*. See or feel the old pattern of stress reactions taken along with it.

Say to yourself:

"This is no longer my reaction and my mind does not replace it with a new habit. I am free."

Imagine dumping the stress along with the reaction that caused it, however you perceive it, into the flow of this graceful, cleansing tide.

The wave begins to move over your head.

Your crown relaxes.

As the wave moves downward your face... your forehead... eyelids... cheeks... jaws... chin and neck relax.

And it keeps moving down your body.

In slow motion, the wave washes over you and through you, slow enough to gather and carry away anything related to a stress reaction.

The wave keeps flowing. Feel the wave move down over and through your shoulders. Then your shoulders and arms become loose and limp. Loose and limp. Not a care... in the world.

Feel the wave washing over and through your torso as it goes... relaxing, releasing all tenseness.

Feel your lower back and spine relax. You are so comfortable... as the wave moves down and through your legs.

Your thigh muscles are loose and limp. Your calves, ankles... feet... loose and limp.

The wave has finally passed over you and through you from head to toe and moved on. You are completely relaxed. Any tenseness from the situation you concentrated upon in the beginning has been carried away.

Relax in your comfort, feeling the peacefulness that's come over you.

Once more, gently visualize the situation with which you began this exercise. Know your mind is relaxed and able to better function to provide answers and results instead of stress.

Think about how calm you feel, how effective you feel. Think about how being calm provides a sense of understanding and confidence. Say to yourself:

"I am in charge of my responses. I am free."

In a relaxed state, you are better able to function. Take a moment and think about how you feel and enjoy the peace that is yours in the most arduous of situations. Simply allow the thoughts to flow without reacting to them.

(Waking From Hypnosis)

Now as I count from One to Ten, you begin to stir from deep contemplation.
One, Two, Three.

As you think about how stress-free you've become, and that you can now remove stress before it claims you, your attention drifts back into this room.
Four, Five, Six.

You begin to stir, becoming aware of your body once again, stretching, breathing deeply, and knowing you now have a personal tool for controlling your reactions.
Seven, Eight, Nine.

Become aware of how wonderful you feel knowing you have a new method of help available to improve your life.
Ten.

Wide awake! Fully alert! You are fully alert!

The Attic Trunk
Finding Your Gifts

For this exercise, choose a person you love who has passed on, someone who might have left behind a gift for you.

Do not choose someone who could harm you.
Do not choose someone you didn't like or who didn't like you.

A gift is not necessarily something tangible. It might be advice they gave that you've forgotten. Maybe it's a special memory.

Whatever turns up in this session, once out of hypnosis, you'll need to interpret how it fits into your life and how it helps you now.

Before you begin, you'll need to know:

1) Climbing a ladder or staircase is symbolic of going up into one's mind or memory.
Opposite of some inductions, you will be counting **UP** from 1 to 5 as you climb up into the attic. You will be counting **DOWN** from 5 to 1 as you climb down the ladder back into the room where you began.

2) Working the lock open is you, opening a place in your mind where you've tucked away what you now seek. You are gaining access to it again.

3) What you find in the trunk is the gift your loved one left for you. It is usually something that helps you as you live your life.

4) If at first you don't understand what you found, don't despair. It has meaning and floats into your consciousness at a most opportune time, most likely giving you one big Aha! moment.

You might simply think through these steps and they may produce nothing surprising. Performing these actions under hypnosis when the mind is accessed and wide open produces stunning results.

A Personal Experience with This Technique: When I performed this technique under self-hypnosis, I was surprised to find my mother's sheet music inside the trunk. I already knew I couldn't become a singer/musician like Mom, though it was my fondest wish. I had long before begun losing my hearing, even as I had already begun a singing gig with a friend in a nightclub.

While entranced, I picked up my mother's sheet music, which was on paper and in music books with paper pages. The feel of her papers, the fact she put things on paper, I believe were instrumental in helping me get started in writing. Some of my creativity today is writing stories and books.

My mind knew I couldn't sing or play music, but produced creativity on paper in the trunk anyway. Although I didn't recognize the message of the gift until sometime later, I always praised my mother's gifts and held them dear, always wondering what the message of that session was. Finally, after acknowledging my desire to write, I realized my mind let me use paper the best way I could put my mother's creativity to use and make it mine.

By the way, Mom's things were stored for years after she passed away. Over a decade later, when my brother was finally sorting through them, he sent me an unexpected package with a note. He wrote: "When I held these, I got the strongest feeling she would have wanted you to have them." What was in the package was all the sheet music and song books my mother kept in her piano bench.

A Huge Caution: I used this procedure of opening a trunk in the attic on a client under hypnosis. We were working to enhance her creativity. She was excited about painting, having innocently dabbled with her daughter's watercolor set and being told that her art showed promise though she felt blocked. What she found in the trunk was frightening to her and she expressed some panic under hypnosis. I simply had her quickly close the trunk and climb back down the stairs.

I gave the suggestion that this experience would be erased from memory like a confusing dream that quickly fades. That is, I gave the suggestion that this therapy session would fade like a forgotten dream. It is not a therapist's position to erase whatever caused her abreaction, but to find it and deal with it. Once examined, any problem either loses its hold over that person or, in the very least, they come to understand it.

Why this happened was because though she wanted to remove the childhood effects of constantly being told she had no talent, she had not been totally forthcoming. She had never revealed to me the fact that she had been molested as a child and that she was presently seeing a psychotherapist for that. She had not mentioned it, nor included it on her written application for therapy with me.

Before you attempt self-hypnosis, be completely honest with yourself and decide if you should be seeing a therapist instead of trying to deal with your issues alone.

The Attic Trunk
Finding Your Gifts
Script

You are deep asleep.

Imagine your loved one has long ago stored something for you in an old trunk in the attic. It fills you with excitement to know that you can now retrieve it

Slowly climb a ladder or staircase leading up into the attic.
Keeping your foothold on the ladder in mind, as well as concentrating on that old trunk. You maintain an air of excitement as you count *slowly* as you go up.

You grip the sides of the ladder with both hands and look up toward the attic opening.
One

Place your foot firmly on the first rung of the ladder and feel the sturdiness of the ladder.
Two

Eager to climb higher, you take the next step.
Three

With the next step, you're high enough to reach up and open the attic access.
Four

You step onto the highest rung.
Five

At the top, poke your head up into the attic and look around and see the trunk. Climb into the attic and go over to it.

(Pause 15 seconds to do this.)

Notice its age and rusted latches. Notice that it glows like a treasure chest. It seems to carry the essence of that wonderful person who's left you something special.

You work with the rusted locks until they break free. If you find them stuck, you work with them until they open.

Slowly open the lid and peer inside.

As you rummage through treasures in the trunk, you find what you're looking for. What do you see?

(Pause 15 seconds)

Pick up the gift and hold it close to your heart. The gift is part of you and has meaning only for you.

(Waking from Hypnosis)

Now as I count from five to one, you begin the five steps to descend the staircase out of the attic bringing your treasure with you.
Five

With your mind filled with excitement over finding your treasure, your attention drifts back into this room as you take the next step down.
Four

Begin to stir, becoming more aware of your body once again... knowing that you have found a long lost treasure that has meaning only for you. You take the next step down.
Three

Become aware of how wonderful you now feel and know you've learned a technique that helps you to remember, helps you to solve some mysteries of your life as you take the next step down.

Two

Now take the last step off the ladder and to the floor, into this room where you began.

Begin to open your eyes, and realize how wonderfully refreshed you are. Now you are wide awake and fully alert.

One

Eyes open. Wide awake and fully alert!

Opening to Creativity

An Actual Hypnosis Session

One of my favorite therapies was to aid people in discovering their unique creativity.

What follows is an hypnotic session of my own, nearly verbatim, where the therapist was helping me unblock my creativity. I always felt stuck when it came to thoroughly expressing in any creative endeavor, as if something were holding me back. I use this as a example of how *imagination* plays a huge part in hypnosis.

The explanations in parenthesis were what we discussed after I was brought out of hypnosis.

I was put into deep hypnosis by a therapist whom I'll call JT.

* * *

JT – Go into your happiest moment when you felt creative. Tell me how you felt.
MD – (I remembered a childhood time when one of my drawings received raves.) I feel high, like I could soar.

JT – Then you aren't afraid of heights? (Attentive he was, immediately picking up on the meaning of my verbiage when I used the word soar. I could simply have left that part off.)
MD – No.

JT – Okay, I want you to imagine a hot air balloon. You're going for a ride that increases the feeling of creative elation. Are you okay with that?

MD – Yes. (Feeling excited, ready for discovery)

JT – First, tell me about your balloon. Describe it's color, how it's made. It's your basket and you created it.
MD – (Mentally, I checked the balloon.) The fire is hot and flowing (symbolic). The balloon is filled with air to keep it aloft (symbolic). The balloon is pink (That surprised me as pink wasn't in my favorite color schemes at the time.) The basket is heavy woven wicker (sturdiness as a basis).

JT – Do you feel safe?
MD – Very safe. It's spacious and comfortable. It's equipped with everything for balloon flying. (Little did I know I was describing attributes of my creative abilities.)

JT – Okay now, it seems you're ready to take off, so see yourself climbing into the basket and see the pink balloon floating ready high above you.
MD – I do.

JT – Now you begin lifting up into the air, slowly at first. As you rise off the ground, do you see yourself lifting?
MD – I do.

JT – Suddenly, something stops you from lifting higher. Do you know what it is?
MD – No. (When he suggested this, I actually felt a light jolt and a pulling feeling, as if being held back.)

JT – Okay, I want you to look around and find what's holding you back.
MD – (I couldn't find anything wrong. Then I mentally looked outside the balloon and to my surprise – even in hypnosis – I saw that one of the ropes that tethered the balloon to the earth had not been released. A symbolic message from my inner self.) Oh, I see.

JT – What do you see?
MD – One of the ropes isn't loosened. I'm still tied down. (I was deep in hypnosis, experiencing – seeing – every detail and action, and enjoying it, I might add, because my mind knew the benefits.)

86

JT – (I heard him exhale, signifying we had found something. This alone told me I was on the right track.) Okay, since this is your balloon, if you want to soar, you need to find a way to disconnect that rope.

MD – (I saw myself and the balloon trying to float higher, pulling against the rope. I was too high to climb out and untie the rope. Instead – and this was all done in my mind because JT told me to find a way to disconnect the rope – I reached into a tool box, got a knife, leaned over the side and cut the rope. These were tools my mind knew would work. I might have exhaled in surprise but hadn't said anything.)

JT – Tell me what happened.
MD – I found a knife and cut the rope.

JT – And now you are lifting again? What's happening?
MD – Yes, I'm soaring! (And under hypnosis, I was. I experienced such a feeling of floating free. It was exhilarating.)

JT – While you are soaring, understand now that nothing keeps you from soaring ever again and you do so any time you wish. Do you understand this?
MD – (It took me a while to focus on his words because I was feeling such elation.) Yes, I do.

JT – (He let me soar a short while. I couldn't say how long.) Okay, now I want you to bring your hot air balloon safely back to the ground.
MD – Okay. (Again, I had to return to a more conscious level of consciousness but still wasn't sure what he was saying. I wanted to remain in the high! Then I feel a coming down feeling and feel the basket touching down. His suggestion brought me down.) I'm down. (I didn't hear exactly that he told me to return. My mind heard it and the thought action brought me to a more conscious state.)

JT – Now, I'm going to bring you out of hypnosis and we'll discuss everything that happened, what it means to you, and how you can use this technique in the future by altering some of it to fit certain situations you may wish to work on. (Thankfully, this therapist spent another half hour with me going over interpretations.)

* * *

This is an example of acting out the suggestions, allowing the mind to conjure the scenario and **trusting** that the help needed presents in the action or shortly thereafter.

What the therapist explained is that I did not need to know what was holding back my creative flow. Under hypnosis, concentrating on freeing creativity, my mind chose a rope, an item used to keep things bound or restrained. Simply cutting the rope was to sever myself from whatever it was that was restraining my creativity. And it worked.

Within a week following this session, my creativity took off in many directions. I began writing the inductions and scripts included in this book, and many more. At that time, I recorded them onto cassette tapes for my clients. Not only did I feel creative, I had no hesitation in what I was doing and no fear of failure.

I will add, that opening my creativity wasn't focused solely on my business of hypnotherapy. Usually for everyone, such freedom generalizes into ALL areas of creativity. My oil painting and photography vastly improved, as did my writing. Now I have written quite a few books and many stories in different genres. To this day I have difficulty keeping myself from becoming involved in too many creative endeavors. An additional benefit was that it's been a great lesson in time management with all I wish to accomplish.

One of my greatest wishes is that others may have the same spectacular results in whatever area they wish to clear and excel.

A WARNING: A potential client claimed she was once a great seamstress, making all her clothing and many pieces for her extended family members. She became emotional when relating how her family enjoyed her sewing for them. She became teary-eyed when talking about having made her daughter's flowing wedding gown. In her application for hypnotherapy with me, she stated that a couple of years earlier a burglar had broken into her home and stabbed her with her very own scissors. She hadn't been able to open her sewing machine since. At the time, she was in private therapy for this. I did not take her as a client.

If you have had severe traumas in your life, please do not attempt self-hypnosis. See a psychologist or psychotherapist to first be freed of the effects of any abuses.

Positive Attitudes

Maintain a positive attitude and thoughts while allowing self-hypnosis to work for you.

Under hypnosis, avoid the use of negative words in suggestions. For example, instead of saying something like, "You will not eat as much sugar anymore," re-phrase it to something like, "You use less and less sugar until you no longer require it in your diet, and that will be real soon." The word *will* puts the action too far off in the future. Another way to word it: "Your eating and drinking habits require minimal use of sugar."

Set a deadline for something you wish to accomplish. Allowing yourself some days or a couple of weeks for the suggestions to begin eliminating your need for sugar, you could say:

"By the end of this month, you no longer desire excessive sugar in your diet."

Keep repeating this in or out of hypnosis. Then let your actions follow your cue. See yourself using one teaspoon of sugar instead of two. Savor the new flavor and equate it with greater health.

A caution here, though: If you are unable to honor promises to yourself, this time constraint suggestion may not work. Self-denial, procrastinating and similar ingrained habits may override any suggestion delivering time constraints. Still, repeat the suggestion frequently.

Instead of saying, "You are not going to argue every time something goes wrong," you might want to say, "When things aren't the way you'd like them to be, you take the time to understand."

Suggestions like this are not going to turn you into a wimp. You're working to change negative habits. The change, most likely, happens gradually but noticeably. If you think your pendulum is swinging too far the other way, you'll naturally adjust long before you've become a dishrag! If anything, you will be much the wiser and happier.

Hypnosis cannot make you do something that is not already part of your character.

Seeking an end to problems is positive. Hypnosis can make you better, more positive. It cannot make you worse unless that is your nature.

Once you've planned a suggestion, put yourself under hypnosis each day and repeat that suggestion. Say it once. Pause a few moments. While waiting, visualize the end result of what you wish to attain. Say it again. Visualize again. Feel yourself already having accomplished your goal. Say it two, three, maybe four times altogether. Concentrate on all aspects of your goal. For example, if it's sugar and dieting, visualize yourself thinner and in new clothes, poised like a model (male or female) for stunning new family photos. Your mind does anything to get you there if you but practice.

End your session at that point. Don't begin to work on another issue. Ideally, work on one issue daily, for perhaps, a month. Then give yourself some time off. After a while, begin to work on another issue, if needed.

If you put yourself under and then spend your session wondering if you're under – Don't! Move right into giving yourself the planned suggestions. Never question it. Just do it.

Work on your self-hypnosis and suggestions daily. What this does is immerse your subconscious in what it is you wish to achieve. That's why, under hypnosis you should think about your goal, feel it, visualize it, and hear it, if sounds are involved. Like getting over the fear of public speaking. Visualize yourself captivating your audience, even if you must see yourself as a speaker you wish to emulate. Feel the attention from your audience. Perceive all these things while you're IN hypnosis. You've heard the saying that if you want to learn something, immerse yourself in everything about it. Use imagination and conjure all the positive elements of what you wish to attain and practice them while in hypnosis.

When we want to learn to do something, we study, read a great and practice. We saturate our minds with what it is we wish to learn. The same principle applies in making hypnosis work for you. While in hypnosis, saturate your mind with positive information and anything your senses can provide about that which you choose to accomplish.

The entire process, beginning your hypnosis induction, applying your suggestions, and bringing yourself out of the hypnotic state can take only a few minutes, *depending on the level of your ability to concentrate*. In the beginning, induction may take a little longer until the idea really sinks in that all you have to do is allow it to work. Keep using the same induction each time. Make your mind know it. Once established, don't change the verbiage of your induction and don't change the verbiage of your suggestions after you begin to use them.

After a while, you get to know the feeling of being entranced and it is that feeling your mind seeks and brings you in. With practice and diligence it becomes automatic. When you relax with the intention of going into hypnosis, that feeling appears immediately as you begin counting yourself in. Simple as that, but it *takes practice*. I reiterate, **it may take a while to reach this ability but it happens with devoted practice because it's a natural ability of your mind.** Your level of concentration is vital. If you have difficulty concentrating in general, I'd like to suggest *concentration* be the first topic you work on under hypnosis.

All people use each of these three means of perception: Visual (sight or imagination), Auditory (hearing), and kinesthetic (feeling). If not visually or hearing impaired, each of us uses one way of perceiving more than the other two.

When giving yourself suggestions to go into hypnosis, if not imagining scenes like a beach or meadow, your might focus on the sounds of the sea and waves lapping. Or you might focus on the breeze flowing across your body. You can rewrite or reword any induction or script to make the best use of your predominate sensory reception.

Then, never mind the outside or unrelated noises you hear. Never mind your stomach acting hungry at the moment it's the best time to start. There are many distractions that present when we decide to do something. **It's simply our mind's subconscious way of testing our commitment to what we're doing.**

Over time our minds have developed a lot of blocks to stop us from doing something. See those blocks as simply tests of your commitment. Focus and concentrate on hypnosis and they disappear.

The following is an advanced procedure. It needs to be performed by a professional, but it confirms that hypnosis in all its forms has much to offer.

* * *

I once attempted to induce hypnosis in a man who would continually clear his throat once we began. He never did that before or after the sessions. However, because of needing to clear his throat, it kept himself in such a light state of hypnosis that he began to doubt his ability to be hypnotized. I then added different verbal suggestions then the first ones I had used with him in earlier sessions to change the induction procedure from one associated with the throat clearing.

Instead of talking him into the trance with only suggestions, I added tapping on the shoulders, touching his hand, gesturing with my hands in slow downward motions, and other gestures he could see while his eyes were still open. My hand movements added impetus to what I was saying – *deeper and deeper*. As he watched me and concentrated on both seeing and hearing, the distraction took him deep into hypnosis. Once I knew he was in trance, I proceeded to work with him and he never cleared his throat again because he didn't realize he was in hypnosis. He thought he was relaxing and getting ready for it.

* * *

This is an advanced technique that therapists use. Of course, it wouldn't work during self-hypnosis, but I use the example here to show how the mind can trick us as it tries to help us. Our minds act up in this manner to test our commitment to what we wish to accomplish. Little preventative nuisances may pop up in your self-hypnosis sessions. Realize what they are and determine to get beyond them by *focusing and concentrating*. After a while this no longer happens once the mind realizes the value of what can be accomplished. It definitely does not happen again when you realize how good it feels to be relaxed and in a trance state where you can help yourself.

Concentrated Concentration

Believing is the key.

I accepted a friend as a client who was curious about using self-hypnosis as an induction to meditation. (More on how this works in the Meditation portion of this book which follows.) While monitoring him as he put himself under, by watching his breathing, I sensed him relax and then he would seem totally conscious again. Then he would relax and then pop out of his trance state yet again. This happened four times. Then he gave up. I found it not only curious but a detriment to his future ability to both put himself under hypnosis or reach a state necessary for meditation.

When we ended the session, I asked why I noticed him floating in and out and never reaching the deeper state necessary for either hypnosis or meditation.

His response was that he didn't feel he was in hypnosis so he would repeat his induction over and over and over again. He had been waiting for some sort of sign to tell him that he had entered an hypnotic state.

Neither hypnosis nor the meditative state comes and rings a bell. It's simply a matter of diligence and believing.

Believe that it's working. Self-doubt destroys any progress made or that can be made.

From the first time you try self-hypnosis, assume you've gone deeply into an hypnotic trance. Believe it! When you've finished your induction, pause and imagine how peaceful you feel. Then immediately begin the post-hypnotic suggestions.

When beginning to practice, you may not be able to tell when you are in hypnosis. To most, it feels like the waking state. People have been led to believe with hypnosis you go into some deep sleep where you know nothing. That is not the case. Simply believe you are in hypnosis and you will be. If you still believe it's not working, be determined enough to go through the complete induction that you started, through a whole Script, and then bring yourself out. How can it possibly work if you stop and deny that it's working? You'd actually be setting yourself up with a post-hypnotic suggestion to fail.

Once out of hypnosis, don't wonder if your post-hypnotic suggestion is going to work. To wonder is to apply more doubt. We don't need to dump a lot of negativity onto good effort. Assume that it's working, as if that's the only way it can happen.

Until you recognize your body's responses under hypnosis, you may not be able to tell you are under. When you are deep in meditation, unlike hypnosis, you may receive many signs.

Induction works for both hypnosis and meditation, but both are totally different states of mind.

Here is one method to add impetus to hypnotic suggestions:

* Once you've pre-planned your suggestion, write it on a piece of paper and stick it onto the corner of the bathroom mirror or maybe on the refrigerator door. Let's say your suggestion is: *You follow a healthy diet every day.* Under hypnosis, give yourself that same suggestion. Doing so gives added instruction to increase the effect in your waking state. Instead of just repeating the phrase under hypnosis, add this cue:

This suggestion is written on a piece of paper stuck to your [bathroom mirror – refrigerator door]. Each time you see that note, the sight of it triggers the suggestion to work in your mind.

With a suggestion like that one, you needn't read the suggestion hanging on the mirror or door. Merely seeing it there is the cue to triggering the original hypnotic suggestion to work. That trigger happens over and over again each time you see that piece of paper stuck in place. It works the same as if you had received the suggestion while under hypnosis. Of course, nothing is lost and more is gained by reading the piece of paper too.

Beside knowing the suggestion is written there, actually reading it drives it deeper into the mind.

To Summarize:

Plan your post-hypnotic suggestion, one sentence, and word it simply in a positive manner.
Memorize it.
Focus or concentrate and induce self-hypnosis.
Believe that it's working.
Mentally give yourself the suggestion and cue.
Bring yourself out of hypnosis believing that it's working.

I like to remind everyone to get comfortable first. Put everything aside that takes your attention. Set a regular time and length of time. Then sit quietly and go through the entire procedure. Know in your mind, there's nothing else you're going to be thinking about.

The secret to learning self-hypnosis and making suggestions work is *concentrated concentration*, intensely focused attention to the exclusion of all else.

Some say they've tried to focus or concentrate and have great difficulty. It happens in meditation too. The moment it's time to still the mind, everything possible begins to float through in a never ending parade! I call this *mind-chatter*.

A technique is available that prevents this from happening. It's called concentration. It's also known as focusing. How many times have you focused on something so intently, you were not aware of anything going on around you? We've all had that happen. That's exactly the same kind of focus or concentration needed to make hypnosis work.

Before you get caught up in thoughts of why self-hypnosis might be too difficult to accomplish even once, let me say this:

For various reasons, most unfounded, we think we have to scour the Universe for answers to things, when in fact, the answers are right here, already a part of us.

If you've been able to concentrate so deeply that you weren't aware of anything else, why then would you look elsewhere to find your concentration when it's already a natural ability?

Having experienced deep levels of concentration, your mind at that moment was preoccupied with whatever you were doing. That is exactly the same preoccupation needed to become adept at self-hypnosis. You've already experienced it. It's easier than you think.

All you need do is focus on your inner voice when performing the inductions and using the scripts or suggestions you've written for yourself. Focusing and concentration, in this instance, are one and the same. Focus on the words, and the meaning of the suggestions. Most of all, believe that it's working, because you can allow it.

Many people may embarrass themselves by blurting out, "Oh, I can't be hypnotized!" It is spoken out of fear; fear of learning what's inside the mind. If you have any kind of mental capacity at all, you can be hypnotized. Many people say they cannot be hypnotized because they're afraid of being made to do something they would not like. Hypnosis cannot—**cannot**—make you do anything that isn't already a part of your morals and ethics. No one can be made to do anything they wouldn't already do. With self-hypnosis or under hypnosis applied by a therapist, you are in charge, therefore you would not give yourself suggestions to do anything against your will. Why would you? Further, if you did, you'd probably pop out of hypnosis and find it difficult if not impossible to go back in at other times.

The only people who cannot be hypnotized are those with no mental capabilities. Some with limited mental capabilities can be hypnotized. When you say you cannot be hypnotized you are saying you do not have any mental capacity.

For those who still say they cannot be hypnotized, the simple fact is the more **intelligent** you are, the more you have control over your mind, the more likely you are to go deeper into hypnosis than others. Therefore, people who have little or no control cannot be hypnotized. The higher your intelligence, the deeper you will go, the more hypnosis will work for you.

The more control you have of your mind, the more you can let yourself relax and allow hypnosis to work for you. No one can control your mind. What you have to gain is that you'll have greater access and control of your mind processes.

An idea or two to consider and help deepen your mental prowess: Listen to your thoughts throughout the day. You could be deeply concentrating at work or at home while preparing dinner, but what about the other thoughts that creep in?

* The neighbor who's become a nuisance.
* Your best friend's stinging advice.
* That guy or girl you liked that turned out to be of questionable character.
* Your failures that keep coming to mind.
* Money problems.

And on and on it goes. Truth is, you more easily manage these dilemmas if you stop thinking about them. Instead, find something to concentrate upon. I'm not talking about a pretty picture or mental image necessarily. Find WORDS that you repeat over and over again in your mind instead of listening to repetitive thoughts that trouble you and drive the worry deeper.

Find a word or phrase to repeat. Say it out loud when alone. That becomes your Mantra. It stops you from spinning your wheels about things you can do nothing about, at least at that moment. The more you think negative thoughts, the more they become ingrained in your mind.

Concentrating upon a pleasant word or phrase stops you from feeling the effect of those actions that caused those thoughts to linger and keep you unsettled.

Find a word or phrase that becomes your mantra. You need not go to a holy person to be given your personal mantra. Many of these people give the same mantra to everyone and then tell them not to tell anyone else. Of course, no one's to know if you don't tell anyone else.

Your mantra is something personal. Perhaps you take great pleasure in improving your mind. You mantra could be something like:

"Your mind is clear now."

Never mind if it isn't yet. By believing that your mind is clear NOW, it becomes so. You may use *"I"* or *"My"* but if you prefer to speak to yourself in the third person, refer back to the instructions for *Self-Hypnosis Induction Explained* to understand why you should speak this way.

A mantra can cover many topics. If you are a gardener and spend your time pulling weeds, but find your mind wanders to things best left alone, your mantra might be:

"Pulling weeds clears your mind."

Focus on what you're doing at the moment and making a positive affirmation of it keeps the mind off intrusions best left alone. Repeat your special phrase over and over till you feel peaceful and find yourself dwelling only on positive topics.

Try to find a phrase not specific to one thing alone that you do. A perfect example is the old adage that was conjured by someone else a long time ago: *Every day in every way, I am getting better and better.* You can use a standard phrase, but most importantly, try to use one that applies to you personally, not only at a time when doing something specific.

Never disclose your mantra to anyone else. It is yours. If you use a mantra like someone else's above, keep it to yourself. You thought of using it or created one of your own. It is pertinent to your life alone. Keep it personal. If someone insists that you've made great changes for the better and wishes to know your mantra, pass them the information presented here and tell them to conjure their own personal phrase, but never reveal yours. It would be giving away your power. Try creating some phrases like these:

* Every day is peaceful now.
* My life runs smoothly now.
* My life is pure joy now.

Life may not be that joyous, but believing that it is moves you quickly to it becoming that way.

Constructing Self-Hypnosis Suggestions

When you take it upon yourself to write your own post-hypnotic suggestions, in order to make them effective, there is the need to learn to construct workable phrases.

Here's a sample suggestion that can be easily worded to align with your way of thinking:

Under hypnosis, dump a headache into a real paper bag and actually throw the bag into the garbage. You would never retrieve something you didn't want from the garbage, so consider it gone.

1) Yes, you can tell yourself that you can move around if the purpose of the hypnosis session calls for it. But don't forget to bring yourself out of hypnosis after you throw the bag into the garbage.

2) Should your headache return, it's a sign of deeper problems. The fact that it comes back is a message to see your doctor.

Almost anyone can learn how to put him or herself into hypnosis. People are finding it easier and easier to do. However, once you've sunk into your hypnotic trance, what exactly do you do next? This is where most people are at a loss. Not knowing what to do, they interpret it as their efforts not really working.

Of course, it's not going to do anything if all you do is get into trance and then sit trying to hold positive thoughts while waiting for something to happen. Positive thinking is great, but you should enter hypnosis for a reason. You should have a script ready to use. Identify a problem you'd like to understand and then choose your Script.

Self-hypnosis, and all hypnosis, functions through post-hypnotic or self-hypnotic suggestions. *Post* and *self* hypnotic suggestions are one and the same, as explained in the *Terminology* section. That is not to say that some changes cannot be automatic. It depends on willingness of the subject and how deep into trance they are able to reach.

When thinking about suggestions you might wish to give yourself once you've entered an hypnotic trance, the first thing you'll want to remember is that **our minds interpret words literally**. Here is an example:

One client proudly confided that he was eager to find his next girlfriend to work on improving his sex life. His past sexual relationships were uninteresting.

"Well, if that's what's important to you," I said.

That man went on to try to prove to me he knew how to handle his hypnosis and suggestions. He said, "I give myself suggestions that my sex life will improve!"

I cringed but hid it from him as best I could. Why belittle someone who came to me for help?

Recalling that our minds take things literally, do you know what's wrong with the wording in his suggestion? He was most likely over-stimulating his libido, which probably didn't need to be, or he wouldn't be concerned about finding a new partner and being more sexually active. He might be stimulating a completely normal libido and not actually dealing with the real problem of why there is no partner in their life. Hypnosis can take a person to *the cause of an issue*. In the case above, it would have been wise for that man to take a good look at his emotional issues, self-denial issues, and so forth. All the things that kept him from build a satisfying relationship. A more workable suggestion would be a general one to begin with. One like:

You are positive about meeting people. You find them rewarding, and you strive to be an open, honest person in dealing with others. You take an active role in building intimate friendships.

When I worked with people having relationship issues, sexuality was not the problem, as some might think.

Emotional issues, fears, phobias and old hurts were the problem. No spouse, mate, or partner can cure these issues in another if that person treats their psychological problems as if they didn't exist. So improving one's sex life doesn't solve much of anything. The root of the problem needs to be indentified and resolved at deeper levels of the psyche. Something else that needs to be examined is why the person chooses to solve a problem without looking directly at it.

In the above case, specific suggestions can be given once the person has taken a good look at what changes occur in themselves from having given those general suggestions about being positive. Strong general suggestions begin to shake loose some of the facade surrounding the problem. Then focus can shift directly onto the problem.

When constructing self-hypnotic suggestions, speak to yourself as if you were speaking to someone else. This is clarified in the section *Self-Hypnosis Induction Explained* where we step away from ourselves. We tend to take ourselves for granted. True, you may be serious about what you're doing, but you may have long ago set yourself into a pattern of taking yourself for granted, letting things slide, procrastinating, self-disbelief. Why would it be different now?

Hidden deep-rooted blocks we have inside our mind-set can seem endless.

If sincere enough to want to help yourself, then a shift in perspectives is in order. Conscious determination to do something about your situation doesn't necessarily erase old patterns. A new perspective is necessary.

Once having learned how to self-induce hypnosis, give yourself only one suggestion at a time. Let's say you want to work on completing all your projects, or work on self-esteem, or work on studying more diligently.

Because these are all varied from one another, you'll want to work on only one issue at a time. Pick one that's most important, whatever your issues may be. Work on that one first.

The following are sample suggestions that have positive effects. See how easy they are to word and suggest? Reword these, if you wish, to your way of speaking.

* You find it easy to complete tasks begun.

* You find it easy to laugh when appropriate. (A suggestion like this would be ideal for a person wishing to cease being a wallflower.)

* You feel great reward when experimenting with your art projects.

Start now. Create a few suggestions of your own. Keep it simple in the beginning. Keep it simple even if you feel experienced at hypnosis.

Section Two:
Meditation

"Meditation is the dissolution of thoughts in Eternal awareness or
Pure consciousness without objectification, knowing without
thinking, merging finitude in infinity."

~ Voltaire

Meditation Introduction

"Even the smallest shift in perspective can bring about the greatest healing."

~ Dr. Joshua Kai, ND

Hypno-Scripts is meant to explain the thin veil that separates the mind processes when accessing hypnosis or meditation. This book deals a lot with hypnosis simply because of the need to rid ourselves of that which keeps us from entering deeper states of mind. When many of our problems and hesitations are eased or removed, and no longer leap to the forefront of our thoughts at the time we wish to concentrate, then meditation can happen spontaneously.

That is not to say that one with severe problems cannot enter meditation. It's a matter of concentration and letting go. Many people find they can meditate to let go of problems. However, meditation is a lot easier and more meaningful and may move us quicker toward Illumination when worldly matters do not distract us.

* Why did you wish to learn meditation?
* Are you simply trying something new?
* Have you already learned that meditation is life changing, always for the better?
* Is it for peace of mind?
* Did someone claim that you could become psychic and that excited you?
* Have you experienced the occult but find yourself ready for the next stage?
* Do you seek the ultimate reward of meditation?

Before attempting to practice the techniques provided to enter into deep meditation, it might be beneficial to become familiar with all that meditation offers (which means additional study beyond this book). It is essential to understand the why of meditation and what is to be gained from the practice. Examples here are but an introduction. Meditation opens doors to spiritual realms. If not prepared for the possibilities, much can come as a shock or even disappointment. Maybe nothing at all will transpire. Become well-read on the topic of meditation offered in books by known and trusted teachers. Avoid those who make wild claims. Be selective.

Learning hypnosis is not essential to learning to meditate.

People who've meditated for years, some all their lives, may know nothing about hypnosis. However with the thin window of the mind separating hypnotic trance and the meditative state, those not successful entering the meditative state now have help to learn how. Hypnosis can facilitate clearing the window to meditation but cannot guarantee Illumination. Achieving the ultimate reward of meditation only happens with commitment, devotion, and *what your level of consciousness can allow*.

For those who've educated themselves a bit and feel they have enough knowledge and are ready to seriously delve into meditation, what is needed is to put aside all that you've learned. Learning is simply mind preparation. Now put aside any pre-conceived notions, desires, and fears about what should or shouldn't happen. Too many people teach that you'll open yourself to negative forces and such. I've never seen this happen to anyone and believe if it happens, it's because the person held these fears and negative thoughts so deeply rooted in the mind it was all they could express. Too, some learn to love the adrenalin rush from living with fear.

Be clear in your mind that you may, with time and devotion, experience a spiritual awakening befitting the level of your consciousness and it will not be negative. True spiritual forces are positive and nothing else.

If using hypnosis to relax into meditation, then please understand the differences between self-hypnosis and meditation techniques as presented in this book:

When giving yourself hypnotic suggestions, your mind remains in a state of readiness to receive instructions. When it's your intention to meditate, be clear of such expectations. Therefore, when using hypnosis to relax into meditation, you may use a cue to free your mind of the sense of readiness and expectation. To do that, after relaxing, tell yourself something like this:

"You now release all expectations and easily slip into meditation using your Mantra."

Meditation cannot be programmed but an hypnotic cue like that serves to turn the mind toward the new direction. At this point, you are relaxed and you would commence using your *Mantra*. Repeating again, once you learn to slip into an altered state, your *intention* is all you need to put yourself into either self-hypnosis or meditation. Can you now see that thin window of consciousness where both are possible and it's your intention that takes you to one or the other?

When either or both self-hypnosis and meditation become a practiced and successful habit, you will slip into either state independently through intention. This is the narrow link and common area between hypnosis and meditation. When intention is pure, whichever you choose to access is attainable. You begin either to count yourself into hypnosis or begin your mantra. Whatever else is to happen begins swiftly.

When first learning meditation, the natural state of mind is to expect nothing. You cannot dictate what you may receive from the all-encompassing greater Power. Some claim to take a problem into meditation and expect an answer or solution. Doing this is simply another form of self-hypnosis, programming a response from the mind.

Meditation goes beyond all expectations of worldly matters of any kind. If there exists an expectation or intention at all, it should be the desire to receive from the Highest realms beyond earthly matters. To the true spiritual seeker, this is automatic. When you may consider taking a desire into meditation is explained as these instructions progress.

An hypnosis technique is useful for clearing the mind-chatter in order to make a mantra work by itself. Eventually the will is strong enough to allow the mantra to work its spell without the continued use of hypnotic suggestions.

Meditation is to enter into a place of stillness, a place of spiritual awareness. Many have tried to quiet the mind only to have all the mind-chatter come at them like someone had turned up the stereo. Many have given up on meditation simply because they never learned to subdue the chatter.

What hypnosis and meditation have in common is that to accomplish turning attention inward, techniques need to be learned to bore the left brain. This was mentioned in the *Standard Hypnosis Techniques Explained* chapter. The logical censuring left brain function monitors day-to-day consciousness. It is that part of the psyche that protects you. It controls the mind-chatter. Numerous techniques to quiet the mind are presented throughout this book, enabling the practitioner to enter deeper states beyond conscious thinking.

Remember: Using cues or mantras repetitively bores the left brain. When the left brain is bored, it turns off. To the left brain there is no reason to protect from a repetitive word or phrase. How wonderfully boring. So the left brain quiets. The mind chatter goes away making a deep state of hypnosis or meditation possible.

While hypnosis is used to affect various situations like changing habits, healing, creativity, and other near limitless possibilities, those same techniques can be used to still the mind for meditational purposes. As with hypnosis using cues to make post-hypnotic suggestions work in the waking state, so can cues, known as mantras to meditators, bring you through the window into meditation.

Why Meditation

Everything we do is infused with the energy with which we do it.
If we're frantic, life will be frantic.
If we're peaceful, life will be peaceful.
And so our goal in any situation becomes inner peace.

~ Marianne Williamson, author of *A Return to Love*

Meditation allows a person to gain control of their life. Sometimes changes in lifestyle are required, letting go of those aspects that keep an aspirant from achieving deeper states.

For a while, some may kid themselves believing they can go out evenings and party hard and then come home and experience deep meditation. Few are that adept naturally.

Truth is, living a fast life with all its actions, mental impressions, raucous sounds, and more, prevents deep meditation no matter how much a person may feel they can achieve in spite of it all.

The mind of the hearty partier may be filled with worldly thoughts, deeds and impressions which are not easily turned off in order to tune in to a spiritually meditative state.

At some point, the person serious about reaching the deepest states of meditation realizes a change of lifestyle is necessary. Changes need not be drastic.

Meditation is gentle and positive. In order to reach deeper levels, live it. Be the person you wish you be but for some reason think you're not. That means to be in a meditative state throughout the day. Saturate your mind with thoughts that promote meditation. That doesn't mean that you walk around in a stupor.

It means:
Expecting peace
Being nice to others
Listening only to positive conversation
Participating in positive endeavors and occurrences
Helping where you can

Giving thanks always for:
Your soul
Your body, your temple
The qualities of your mind
Your desire to elevate your consciousness
The progress you've already made
Your peace of mind

Ask for:
time to meditate
strength to stick to a routine
direction in the steps toward enlightenment

Daily living affects consciousness and can distract from the depth of our trances. Calm desires about always needing things happening around you. Abstain from extreme excitement or anger. When control is gained over emotions and desires, a *huge* step in releasing that which prevents meditation is achieved.

Too, get enough exercise and eat right to keep not only the body but the brain healthy. It is through this magnificent instrument that meditation is able to bring all things into being.

A Word about Drugs and Alcohol

I've never experienced recreational drugs. Early in my life I learned I have severe allergic reactions to some prescription drugs and to most all alcohol. I have counseled people who claim their best meditations happen when they're on a drug induced high. Yet, when they describe what they experience in these drug or alcoholic states, it ends up being nothing more than hallucinations. The mind needs no exterior induced stimulants. You come equipped internally with all that you need.

True meditation, reaching the highest possible level—or the deepest, whichever way you see it—happens naturally with proper training and direction. No extreme stimulants are necessary.

You come equipped with all you need to reach the states of mind progressing you toward Illumination. You accomplish this without added stimuli. All human beings come so equipped. Many have been looking in wrong places, have not been educated about their potential, or live in denial because of programming that inadvertently seeps in according to the lives lived.

**"The soul is the same in all living creatures
although the body of each is different."**

~ Hippocrates

To Hippocrates's words I would add that while the soul is the same and the body is different, so are the paths different that each takes toward self-realization, depending on how society and culture affects us. We have choices we need to make.

So, be a little humble. Be assertive when a situation calls for it, maybe aggressive if necessary, but realize a Power greater than all exists perpetually. Those who believe they are greater or more important before they comprehend that fact, will never understand the level of greater power humankind is capable of attaining.

Caution: As you become adept, you may wish to tell family and friends. You may wish to spread the word of the Truth and validity of these practices. Be aware that when people know what you're doing, and as your reputation as a mediator or advanced practitioner spreads far and wide, you may be approached by people offering what they feel is confirmation.

One such person approached me and said the reason I was so adept was because I was from Atlantis and had already developed my powers back then, and had come back to help the general populace uplift consciousness. This was not information of any kind other than the speaker's attempt to validate her own belief system. I have heard lots of similar statements and simply asked the Powers That Be that they stop, and they did. People casting frivolous comments about like this are what give the entire realm of spiritual existence a bad reputation.

The message here is to be discerning of what you hear or read. If a person would have you believe they are highly evolved and that allows them to make such statements, don't walk, run away. If persons making such unsought statements are so highly evolved, they would not be making flippant remarks such as these.

The true professional would allow you to uncover such Truths about yourself, and not simply throw them at you. Other more professional means exists to reach people.

Be discerning in what you place your beliefs and importance. If not from a professional, follow your intuition. Intuition is another inner quality that never harms you. It is your higher self guiding you. In being discerning, you will also meet people like you with whom you may share.

Meditation Progress

Some of my early experiences made me the thankful seeker I am today. The effect of sitting still as a toddler has stayed with me my entire life. It was a way of entering an hypnotic state. It naturally led into meditation. Or had I been doing both at once? The white lights I focused upon behind my eyelids intensified throughout my life and have become much more.

Knowing the overall confirming effect it has brought, I wish to help others experience these advanced steps and the Illumination that meditation brings.

No one need be a lifetime meditator to benefit from meditation. Begin at any age.

Back when I was about thirteen, I began more clearly seeing colors in those white drifts, as discussed in the chapter *Unintentional Childhood Training*. I thought I had seen colors prior to that time but paid them no mind. Then the hues intensified.

Again, it was all normal for me. Several times through my teen years, I hinted at or mentioned this phenomena to one friend or another with whom I felt rapport. Each time, those friends had no understanding of what I spoke.

I began to wonder if something was wrong with me or maybe with my sight. The strange self-doubting thoughts that traipsed through my mind were many, but I still knew I would be okay. I don't know how I knew that. For a while, it was confusing for me at that age. However, I lived with my secret because it made me feel good and hadn't killed me! Nor had it affected my sight. Not knowing what to make of it all, it remained my secret. Somehow I knew I would not be harmed by any of this.

I did tend to withdraw a bit or friends labeled me as withdrawn sometimes. That was because I could see that swirling with my eyes open, seemingly in the air in front of me! It didn't always happen. When I was in a deeply pensive state, day-dreaming or in a light meditative state I would see it openly.

In my early teens, I began seeing a distinct purple or blue/purple that appeared in an area a little higher than looking straight out. At times it was pure deep blue; other times true purple. These colors came and went among the usual pale ones which eventually faded and I saw them no more. The blue/purple always pulsated, moved around, had ever-changing shapes and blotches, came forward and then receded, as did all the lights and colors I saw. The blue/purple blotches became so strong over time I could only marvel at their brilliance. The hues weren't brilliant like a neon sign, but they were the most stunning shades of those colors imaginable. The blue/purple was not regular at first. It appeared and disappeared of its own accord. I would wait and sometimes it wouldn't appear. As time passed, and with regular practice, it became constant and has been since. The meaning of seeing these lights is discussed after the techniques included here that lead, hopefully, to your own light show.

Not until I was into my early thirties and meeting people also practicing meditation did I begin to understand with what I had been blessed to receive. I studied, read hundreds of books, and all confirmed I was on the right path. With in-depth studies, phenomenal occurrences began happening in my life. I became more psychic. I had numerous out of body experiences, dreamed in foreign languages, and heard sounds and smelled odors I couldn't identify. I saw things and knew things, some of which I wish I never perceived.

I experienced a multitude of paranormal occurrences while trying to learn more about what this phenomena of lights meant for me. It was a time when my blue/purple swirls began to take shape and become nearly solid, sometimes round, sometimes oval and always casting off brilliant emanations. Needless to say, everything that I experienced could fill a few books. What I learned was that these paranormal occurrences are stages in learning and development that any person may experience. Some people may not experience any of this. Those frightened by experiences such as these should have no fear. It sometimes becomes a matter of what you hold strongest in your mind.

Simply because some people fear them, don't want them, or don't believe in them, they probably will not experience much phenomena no matter how adept they become at mediation if attracted to practice at all.

What's necessary to know is that the psychic and phenomenal realms are but steps on the path of one's enlightenment. It is not a place to get stuck. It is not a place to linger. So you become psychic. So you have phenomenal experiences. Let it all pass. They are but rungs on a ladder you climb to get to the top.

To become fascinated and hold one's self at these levels is to stunt evolutionary progress. Let them pass, if you experience psychic phenomena at all. What it amounts to is mind-clearing, mind-conditioning, getting past those abilities we all have to some degree; and they can glut the mind.

A few people can function in the psychic realms without stunting their growth. It may be an ability that was pre-ordained for them.

Some reading this may have heard of the internationally known trance medium, Kevin Ryerson. Kevin was a member of our group in Arizona for a time back in the 1970s. Back then, he admitted that he had found his psychic ability as he was practicing learning self-hypnosis. I long ago lost touch with him so cannot attest to how he's progressed spiritually or beyond the psychic realms. Actually, he was a spiritual person when I knew him.

Eventually, I found people experiencing the shifting clouds behind the eyelids. Mine came naturally simply by closing my eyes. Then, as the phenomena became more widely known and desired – as people rushed trying to elevate their consciousnesses – some were trying to make the cloud and lights happen manually.

In meditation groups I saw people with eyes closed actually applying pressure to their eyeballs in an effort to produce the clouds and lights. I was frightened for those people. Applying pressure to the eyeballs causes serious impairment and irreparable damage not only to the eyeball but to sight itself.

Many people used what is called a *beragon*, a T-shaped arm support on which they rested their elbows in order to apply constant pressure to the eyeballs during their entire meditation period. While it is true, the Hindus use a beragon on which to rest their arms, they use it for applying fingertips to numerous nerves or pressure points around the eye orbits and it definitely doesn't wreck the eye sight.

Too, if one must remain conscious enough to keep applying pressure for the sake of seeing some phenomena, what depth of meditation could they possibly reach?

* * *

Meditation cannot be induced manually. It is an ability of the inner mind or the soul when conditioned and trained correctly, and when conditions that prevent us from seeing our true nature are removed.

* * *

Spirit light is not something that can be induced manually or by any physical means. Neither is it something that can be programmed to happen under hypnosis. Any effort to make phenomena happen only becomes a barrier to the natural process.

Early on, I learned that meditation for me was best when it was dark. It seemed to enhance the sight and activity of the lights I saw. I had always gone to bed early from childhood. As a result, for most of my adult years, I wake in the wee hours between 2:00 to 4:00 a.m. Many teachers of meditation tell aspirants to meditate in the morning when fresh and rested. I had been doing this all my life.

After my morning sessions – about an hour each – I'm ready and energized to start my day. I do, however, often meditate during daytime whenever I feel like tuning in. Daytime produces differences in the phenomena, but looking for the phenomena is not the true purpose of meditation. What you do with your experience as the ability deepens is what matters.

Eventually, I was told by a holy man that the blue/purple lights a person sees is the essence of their soul. I have looked deep into the eyes of several holy men, and they into mine, and they all verified the same and I am humbled.

About Mantras

Cues and mantras are discussed throughout this book, but be clear about your intention when deciding which state to enter, hypnosis or meditation, and which technique to use.

Notice here that I try not to use phrases like *will happen* or *should happen*, (though in few instances it's necessary.) These tend to be programming language and it is not my intention to program anyone. I wish all to have their own experience absent of any programming that simple yet powerful words, thoughts and practices can bring about.

A mantra is a word or short phrase repeated usually mentally which eventually stills mind-chatter, promotes relaxation, and helps to deepen the state of mind moving toward self-realization.

Many people take classes with a guru or holy person. They spend numerous dollars and many hours preparing for a time when the guru will finally award them a mantra. This is well and good because those people learn much about stilling the mind for meditation. They learn about its purposes and what they might achieve. Yet, what is offered here is a way for those serious enough to begin the journey by themselves to still the mind and reach a state of quietude. Only reaching that point does a person move forward toward self-realization.

As discussed under *Mantras* in the *Terminology* section and in several chapters, try to find a word or phrase that is yours and yours alone.

What follows is a short example from my experience with identifying both a cue and a personal mantra, one I discovered after a therapist/teacher said something to me privately.

* * *

By using hypnotic regression on myself was I finally able to understand my affinity for the number 6. I have always thought my favorite number was 8, maybe 9, but 6 always popped into my mind when I wished to choose. When putting myself in hypnosis and counting backwards from 10 to 1, I begin to feel the depth of my induction once I reach the number 6.

In one self-hypnosis session I had an Aha! moment when I realized it was something the therapist said to me when he was putting me into trance back in the late 1960s. The four simple words, including the number 6, that he said as he touched my forehead (a confirmation that I was deep in trance) has become one of the cues I use to take myself deeper into hypnosis. It has become one of my persona mantras. When I am counting myself into hypnosis and reach the number 6, I say those four words he said to me and Wow! I'm under. Continuing on from there to number 1 takes me deeper still.

* * *

While being a fledgling at anything, you are most vulnerable. When you tell someone what you are doing and they laugh, disagree, or give a lot of negative feedback as to why they don't believe in what you are doing, you become deflated and discouraged. Their negativity weakens you because you have given away your power. Whether fledgling or accomplished, guard your cue or mantra as something sacred.

If you wish to create your secret mantra, think of something you can easily repeat that has meaning for you only.

Some examples to avoid:

* Your child's name or any person's name: Meditation is personal to the exclusion of all others.
* Pets: Same reason as a person's name.
* City, town or place names: Paris may have been lovely, but don't bring any worldly essence into your meditation. When used this way, you invite too many memories into your meditation.

* Healing from illnesses: Do not mention sickness or disease. A mantra phrase like *healing from cancer* is not a mantra. It's a goal to accomplish. Mentioning a disease repetitiously may only prolong it or make it worse. Likewise, do not mention grave illnesses when changing the *Allergy Control Script* to suit your needs.

Anything with a worldly connotation should be avoided. Meditation is a mind-state apart from worldly influence.

Some good examples:

* A word or phrase that may change your life for the better: It needs to be short in order to retain concentration on it. Something like *pure mind, pure heart*.

* The word *Love*: That term has different meanings for different people, so maybe too broad in scope.

* The word *Om* or *Aum*: Widely used in meditations.

> "AUM or Om is not related to any religion
> because Om was practiced before the birth
> of all the religions of the world."

> ~ Amit Ray, *Om Chanting and Meditation*

If your phrase has a worldly connotation, find a different mantra.

A mantra can be something you concentrate upon speaking or seeing IN YOUR MIND, though this seems to happen naturally once you are well-grounded in your practice. You can program your mind with a mantra, or if adept, your mind may simply supply one.

* Imagine thin wispy white clouds drifting past: Your imagination helps to bring in that which eventually appears on its own.

* Colors: See only white, yellow/gold, blue, or purple in muted or pastel shades. You'll understand more about color as I describe what they mean later in this Meditation section.

* White light beaming down from the Heavens: What could be better?

* A deity if you have one: Let it be the highest of your belief system so you won't be focusing on a statue or idol sitting on your dresser, which is only a material object, a worldly replication.

* A repetitive sound: The quiet ticking of a clock is relaxing to some while others find it obnoxious.

* * *

A HUMOROUS NOTE: When I was a child and using my form of meditation, anytime my mother would start the vacuum, the steady hum would put me into a trance. I'd rush to the sofa to sit and be still. Mom thought I was simply putting my feet up and getting out of her way. To this day, any steady hum has a calming effect on me. I don't even mind leaf-blowers. And, no, I do not go into trance when I vacuum. Or maybe....

* * *

A mantra for meditation may be one word, like saying the word Om on a long exhaled breath. It may be a phrase relating to something spiritual in nature. No one needs to be a religious person in order to learn and benefit from meditation. All that's required is that you be loving in your heart.

Several ways exist to finding your mantra:

You can enter hypnosis and ask that you be given one. After asking, your mind may throw something out to you immediately. Or it may come to you the next day or the next. Maybe you already know what you wish to use. Then go into your hypnosis and give it life. That is, under self-hypnosis, tell yourself that special mantra takes you into deep meditation. Don't forget to repeat that mantra when under hypnosis. Keep the verbiage simple. Repeat it two or three times while under hypnosis and stating that it is your mantra for meditation. That's all. Then begin using the mantra each time you wish to go into meditation.

Something wonderful about a mantra is that you can repeat it during the waking state. You can say it to yourself all day if you wish and you will not go into meditation on the spot. You will not go into meditation till it is your *intention* to do so. Repeating your mantra over and over and over clears the mind-chatter. You'll find your thinking becomes clearer, your countenance more peaceful.

Breathe Into Meditation

Breath is life. Think of breath as the glue of our being, that which holds body and soul together. What we inhale is the ether that sustains all of life. Why not make each breath count, using it to help us reach the human potential of Illumination, which is the goal of living.

We breathe predominantly from one nostril or the other. The breathing period from either nostril lasts about an hour before the sides switch autonomously. One brief period exists during the switch when we breathe from both nostrils at the same time.

When intending to meditate, breath is something to concentrate on for only a brief few moments. Once your practice is established, the few initial breaths become automatic, as does proper breathing.

Be in a time and space where you are not rushed, where you are comfortable and can stay for an unspecified amount of time without interruption of any kind.

* Sit with your back straight as possible or lie down.
* Unless sitting in a lotus or cross-legged half lotus, do not cross your arms or legs.
* When lying, have your arms at your sides, not on top of your body. Try to lay flat, not having 3-4 pillows scrunched up behind your head.

HELPFUL TIPS:

1) In meditation it is essential to keep the spine as straight as possible due to the flow of energy that sweeps through the nerves and affecting the entire body.

2) When laying flat, if you notice your back or spine becoming tired or uncomfortable, slowing and gently lift one leg, bending sideways at the knee, and place the sole of that foot against the inside of the opposite knee. That would resemble the lower half of the Tree Pose in Yoga. That shifts the spine just enough to provide great relief and allow you to remain peaceful a while longer.

One of Many Easy Breathing Techniques: Repeat this technique three times. Some have to build up to the length of time that's best. Many books have been written about breath in meditation; many books include the information among myriad other topics. This is only one technique and the easiest to perform.

Focus up between your brows.
Take a long, deep breath. If you can, inhale to the count of 8.
Hold for the count of 4.
Exhale to the count of 12.

You may begin to feel light-headed or like you're floating. That's okay, it's only three breaths and any dizziness passes. After three repetitions, allow your breathing to return to normal in a slow, gentle flow.

Begin to repeat your mantra, slowly and without effort. It's best to say it in your mind. Speaking out loud tends to not only take effort, it holds you in a perpetual state of conscious awareness when it's best to simply let go.

Once your mind-chatter is turned off, you may feel deeply relaxed. Keep gently repeating your mantra.

Expect nothing.

In the beginning, focus on nothing except, perhaps, the darkness in the backs of your eyelids. When you first close your eyes, you may see white swirls behind your eyelids that cease in one or two minutes. These are simply impressions cast off by the retina or nerves. You easily learn the difference between these and the meditation lights and swirls. These first sightings end long before the real ones begin.

Let any thoughts that come to mind float away. If need be, actually see the words of your mantra floating through your mind, and then see those disruptive thoughts disappearing into the distance. Focus on your mantra.

You may find that you eased off and stopped saying your mantra. Begin again, gently, because you had slipped into a state of meditation though you didn't know it. When you floated out again is when you noticed you had stopped saying the mantra. Simply start again. In time you recognize the feeling of meditation, are able to hold yourself there, and repeating the mantra can be stopped until again needed.

For the duration of time set aside for meditation you may think that thoughts kept interrupting and you spent the entire time pushing them aside. This happens to most beginners. You may spend several sessions like this until you condition your mind to let go for meditation. In a sense, repetition of your mantra teaches your mind to obey what you wish to accomplish.

* * *

Have you noticed that when in a group, perhaps in a large room full of people and all need to settle down and become attentive, many begin clearing their throats? You can hear it from different people all around the room. This is one way the mind asks if you are ready for what's about to happen? It's the same with mind-chatter popping up when entering hypnosis or meditation. At the moment you need to settle in is when your attention is called to your mind-chatter. Focusing on your mantra to the exclusion of all else leaves no room for other thoughts and stops the mind from its tricks.

Your session is over if you have spent enough time allowing meditation to come to you. Many people give up after five minutes because they cannot control the mind-chatter. Try to set aside, perhaps, one-half hour and stay in that one-half hour to give yourself fair chance to accomplish what you intend. You'll be amazed at how fast one-half hour passes and you'll wonder where you were during that time. Regardless you thought you spent it trying to clear your thoughts, you were in light meditation.

NOTE: Most people do not perceive the qualities of meditation until they have practiced for some time and then finally recognize the differing states between meditation and wakefulness. The meditative state is easily recognized with practice. Usually those reaching that state find themselves hungering for it, seek it, learn its positive ramifications, and never let it go.

Ending the Meditation

Unlike self-hypnosis where it's wise to count yourself back to a full waking state of consciousness, meditation does not require this. In fact, meditation leaves you with such a peaceful countenance that you may keep it naturally after ending your session.

All you need do to end a meditative session is to open your eyes and orient yourself to your surroundings. Check in with how you feel. Take a moment to go over what you perceived about the session. Do not allow doubt and negativity to creep in. Simply give thanks that you have had the time to do this; give thanks for progress made. Great progress is made with each and every session.

Many people come out of their sessions feeling they went somewhere but can't describe it. Truth is, they had gone into a deeply relaxed state or simply dozed off. However, the purpose of meditation is not to space out into some unknown zone in order to get away from life's ills. The accomplished meditation practitioner recognizes the meditative state and remains conscious and aware throughout the time they are entranced. Much happens in the conscious meditative state. This is discussed as you read further.

Some beginning mediators recognize they can reach a meditative state easily or almost instantly. That is, most likely, because they have read a lot to increase their knowledge of what meditation is and is not and it has conditioned their minds. Some may be already practicing Yoga or Tai Chi Tuan and other modalities that require a degree of mind control and the ability to concentrate. If you wish to educate yourself to help reach a meditative state easily and quickly, saturate your mind with information about meditation. Become your meditative state. You may never go back to being the person you were without it.

Bring In Help

"Spiritual progress is like detoxification."

~ Marianne Williamson

When beginning your session, instead of focusing on your interior, try this outer technique with white Light.

Visualize yourself surrounded with strong white light, like being inside a cocoon. Let it remain through your entire meditative session. You needn't worry that it may disappear when you turn to other thoughts. See it there first.

If it's difficult to imagine being surrounded with that cocoon, then think about the religious images seen in pictures where a halo of light hovers over the tops of their heads. Imagine that kind of light and make it gold or pure white and glowing. That is the light with which to surround yourself. See it at the top of your head and then let it expand and drop down like a sheath around you.

Then, still not focusing inward, imagine a beautiful glowing white cloud floating overhead, way up in the atmosphere. Watch it drift. It's never ending and it's beautiful.

Focus on it.

That pure essence is the Universal Ether. It is where all ideas, all inventions, all creativity, everything good that is known to the human condition originates.

You've heard the term, *"All things happen at once, in the blink of an eye."* Maybe you've heard, *"All ideas come from the Universe for anyone to tap."* Acknowledge this and wait patiently and then let go of the thought.

Next, open your mind like a funnel at the top of your head. A white funnel of light ready to receive. Imagine it wide open.

You are unique. You have special gifts to give to the world.

Open to them to acquire them. The deeper mind is where to connect with all your talents. In a sense, allow them to find you. They will pour into your funnel.

So imagine the gifts that are yours originating out there somewhere. Never try to dictate what gifts you wish to receive. Simply realize that you were created with special purposes. Whatever is yours attracts to that funnel and to your mind.

Next, imagine the pure white Essence beginning to pour down into your funnel, down into your mind. When this happens, simply wait in thankfulness. Simply wait and allow what happens. When finished, the Light may pull away, but will return anytime you wish.

You may most likely have no idea what you've received. However, if you are trying to accomplish something in your daily life, you may within hours, days or more, realize you had the answer all along.

* * *

The first time I performed this technique, tears poured out of my eyes though I didn't feel I was crying. Later, a therapist told me it was a spiritual cleansing.

After meditation deepens, enter this type of meditation with a specific problem you wish to solve. Expect a resolution from the Universal Ether, but never dictate what you are to receive. You may have a problem you'd like to see resolved a certain way and may expect help in making the resolution happen. However, the universe may bring resolution unlike anything imagined. The reason you could not solve your problem is because you may have been expecting the wrong solution. It may come in the days that follow in a way not to your expectations, but in the end you will be amazed how your problem resolves and you will feel thankful for it.

Many books teach that you can manifest your wildest dreams through practicing meditation. While it is true many dreams come to fruition, I am uncertain about what many people harbor as their wildest dreams and so heap disappointments upon themselves when expectations are not met.

If it is your wish to bring many of your dreams into fruition, I encourage you to read more. Find books that give techniques to bring this about.

What we're accomplishing here is simply to open the mind to meditation without necessarily dictating what can or cannot happen. The mind is limitless, as is its power, but it needs to be opened. When tapped, anything can happen. Placing yourself in meditation is to open the door to your higher self.

Read
Study
Practice
Change your life
Stay humble

Old and New Collide

In the early 1970s I was active with a group of like practitioners. I was still searching for my true self and developing. My son was eleven years old then and sometimes attended meetings and meditations with me.

Among our group was a man who had many years earlier lost the fingers of one hand. Still he was a psychic artist. He would sit quietly with his pastels and velvet papers during the get-togethers. He would draw images he saw in his mind, either from people around him or, as he said, "...from the faces that pop into my mind." When the meetings were done, people among the attendees would find he had drawn a relative or close friend who had passed on. He also drew spirit guides.

On a different evening at home I sat in deep meditation. Suddenly and surprisingly, I dropped into a dark space. I didn't know where I was until a lighted area opened out. I saw that man, the artist, sitting with my young son at a desk. I knew that man was teaching my son to draw. Then the man saw me.

He sounded a little perturbed and said, "You're too early." I began to withdraw. Then he said, "Wait, take this and concentrate on it till it's your time."

What came floating toward me were two regular cupped hands. They held what looked to be a chunk of gold fashioned into another hand, but the golden hand had no fingers! On the palm of the golden hand, designed by the lines on the palm, were traces of faces.

The message of the meditation was clear and proved out immediately. Within days, my son began to draw and use colored pencils. I still have his stunning art. I should bring it out of storage and frame it.

Within days of him starting I, too, began to draw. I began my artistic endeavors by drawing faces that surprisingly popped into my mind. I still have those drawings as well. Since that time many years ago, my creative abilities have expanded beyond anything I could then have imagined.

A recent revelation came as another Aha! moment though it shouldn't have been surprising. I was reading the book, *The Quantum Prayer: An Inspiring Guide to Love, Healing, and Creating the Best Life Possible*, by Dr. Joshua Kai, ND. One of the techniques he offers to effect change is to hold a seed of light in the palm of your hand and concentrate on it, imbuing it with all the good that is yours and is to come. There is more to the stunning technique that I won't go into here. However, it's serendipitous that Dr. Kai instructs to hold a light in the palm of your hand and focus on it. Decades ago I focused on the golden hand that was offered in the two cupped hands, and look where it's taken me. Some techniques have been around for eons because they work. We've only to open ourselves to receive them.

What Do You See?

"To understand the immeasurable,
the mind must be extraordinarily quiet, still."

~ Jiddu Krishnamurti

Many people never disclose what they perceive in the meditative state. Meditation is extremely personal. Though it's advised to keep an open mind and not ask for or expect anything from meditation in the beginning, during a group session....

One person may only practice breathing.
Another will go into a deep trance.
One may see visions.
Another may pray.
One may use the period to establish affirmations.
Another may appeal to their deity.
Some try to commune with spirit guides.

The reasons seem endless. Never expect the true meditator to tell you about his or her experiences. It's simply too personal. However, I will share some of mine, additional to the experiences I wrote about in the chapters *Unintentional Childhood Training* and *Meditation Progress.*

As a child as early as two years old, I began to see those swirling white lights in the blackness behind my eyelids. Over the years they became brighter and brighter and I began to see pale hues in them. My fascination was such that I could not stop watching nor expecting them.

As mentioned earlier, in my teens, I began to see brilliant blues, blue/purple, but the pinks and yellows faded. During one meditation, the blue/purple light started as a pinpoint of white light and then burst open in that stunning blue/purple, so fast and bright it startled me. It rushed over me like someone throwing a bucket of water over my head. I physically felt it douse me. I popped out of meditation then.

When I sat for my next session, I was faced with having to deal with this brilliant light because it was vastly different from the others. I didn't know what it meant and had been left feeling it had a life of its own, but it was beautiful. I didn't feel anything negative about it. In fact, I wanted to see it again!

Since then, among all that brilliant white light, I have always had the blue/purple light swirling and receding, moving about in the darkness I perceive as my natural meditative state. Several times through the years, I received more dousing.

In my late teens and early twenties, life took some strange turns and I found myself neglecting my sessions. I am not claiming that the absence of my sessions caused me to endure great hardship and several times nearly lose my life, but life got confusing. Meditation was put aside. Yet, every time I closed my eyes, if only to go to sleep, the lights were there. Not knowing what to do with them, not that we're to attempt dictating what's to be done with them, I watched them a while and let them be and usually slipped into sleep though my mind was troubled. If anything at that time, those lights were constant and brought me great comfort.

During my twenties, I noticed my intuitive growth. As a child, I'd already had some psychic experiences, like telling my mother her father would soon pass. That was hard on both of us, for obvious reasons. I'll say mostly it was intuitive hunches that played out, like knowing when people were going to die by the way that they smelled, and I was always right. Death wasn't all that I perceived but it was some of the most serious. Usually occurrences that carry the most emotion are easiest to perceive. I experienced a lot of pleasurable premonitions, too, and my dreams have offered premonitions.

So I found myself becoming psychic and hid it because some of the first things I heard were that I would be labeled a New Age wannabe or even a charlatan. Yet, I was honest and sane and knew it and knew only I could keep my reputation clean.

As these occurrences kept happening to me, I began to read and study, always relying on meditation to keep my mental/spiritual equilibrium. A few years passed as I found myself gaining more and more abilities that many people shunned. But the universe – or consciousness – conspires to help. Eventually, I found new friends experiencing the same shifts in consciousness. What a joy!

More years passed and I learned to look beyond the psychic realms. I came to realize these abilities are quite natural for the true seeker accessing deeper states of mind. Yet, I sensed more to this phenomena, more to life, and fascination with these psychic abilities were holding me back. Finally, I plunged back into a deep meditational practice. I had never abandoned it, but maybe took it for granted.

During the years I was learning about being psychic, practicing some of my abilities and generally opening psychically, I always had the feeling something was missing or that I was missing the point of it all. What I wished to accomplish in life wasn't coming my way. The things I wished to do were always out of reach. My psychic ability seemed to work for others but not for myself. So I clung to my meditation practice, feeling the answers lay therein, and watched the psychic realm and that type of phenomena recede to the background my life. Many people opening to a hypnosis or meditation practice may experience being psychic to some degree. How far each person wishes to take it is a matter of personal preference and motivation.

With the new commitment to meditation, suddenly I began meeting people who could help me understand and to attain some of my goals. I began to feel great relief and wasn't sure why. Then I realized with the psychic realm comes a lot of responsibility. A psychic person takes on a lot of obligation when they feel motivated to tell others what they perceive about them. Some people fear what they may find in their own minds. What is more unsettling is what a psychic perceives in the minds of others. A psychic can help numerous people if that be the path they choose in life.

Yet, while being psychic may help some people – and greatly hinder others – my life was wrapped up in others who should seek on their own. I always felt something was missing. I was neglecting my true purpose. Myself. In meditation I sought guidance for what was to come. My inner search didn't go unrewarded. It was life-changing.

135

It was as if I had to experience all that phenomena, know that realm in order to recognize what came next. I didn't need to be psychic to make my life work. I didn't need to keep myself at one stage in order to feel this lifetime was worthwhile – or believe that I might have to reincarnate and pick up where I left off before I could reach Illumination.

I'm still a bit psychic but it's become integrated into the facets of my life. The blue/purple lights are stronger still. While they came sporadically over the years, they now appear with each and every meditation session and I sometimes see them in broad daylight with my eyes open.

In the beginning, I said we shouldn't ask or expect anything of meditation. However, being a regular meditator can make things happen that you hold dear, and you don't have to ask. Eventually, wishes for meditational advancement are fulfilled without effort on your part except for your devotion. Advancement may not happen overnight, but when the heart is in alignment with higher consciousness, the connection made during meditation can affect changes never before thought possible.

Think of the possibilities if the whole world understood meditation and the powers of the deeper mind.

Early on, I reminded that your mind should be free and clear of wants and desires when entering meditation. This is true, but having established a practice and using it faithfully, you can take a wish or desire into meditation. Do so and then **let it go**.

The problem with taking expectations into meditation before your practice is established is that most people keep looking for an instant result. They want meditation to immediately give them what they asked for. So they go about their days waiting and waiting and then deciding meditation doesn't work after all.

Do not expect anything till your practice has deepened and you have received signs that it has. Still, expect nothing, and then be awed when you realize the results that happen when all expectation is put aside.

It's been my experience that a light state of meditation is not where those wishes can be acted upon. Deepen your meditation and be committed.

You know when meditation is deepening by the way life in your normal waking state changes for the better. You might find your wishes coming true. You might simply feel much happier.

It's more like a feeling that comes over you, a revelation, though you may not know why. You may know by the lights that may appear during your quiet times. You know intuitively without having to consciously think about any it. Trusting the process and having faith in yourself is all-important. Trust is what allows progress to happen swiftly. It's about knowing you have accomplished something special and you simply go with it.

Understanding Those Lights

The swirls of light behind the eyelids come to those practicing intense focusing in the meditative state. It's like confirmation that may bring tears of joy, knowing they are accomplishing that which they set out to do, and knowing that they are elevating their consciousness. Some see the phenomena without practice. This is due to the level of consciousness at which they dwell.

If none of this happens for you, you must not give up. Inner peace is what meditation brings. If you consciousness is such that you do not experience these states, devotion to your practice will bring you closer to it. Regular meditation will be elevating your level of consciousness.

The light we see is the essence of our souls. Everyone has a soul, including those who choose not to believe it.

* * *

In the book *Hands of Light: A Guide to Healing Through the Human Energy Field*, the late Barbara Ann Brennan, says:

"No, you are not going crazy. Others are also hearing noises from nowhere and seeing lights that aren't there. It's all part of the beginning of some wonderful changes taking place in your life in a perhaps unusual but most natural way.

"There is abundant evidence that many human beings today are expanding the usual five senses into super-sensory levels. Most people have High Sense Perceptions to some degree, without necessarily realizing it. Most can develop them further with earnest dedication and study."

* * *

Whatever degree of High Sense Perception you may have could be subconsciously pushing you to expand your awareness and your consciousness.

Mentioned in Brennan's quoted material is that the practitioner may hear various noises and sounds. Let them pass. They are a product of the mind. Their meaning may or may not be known. They are simply a product of changing consciousness. Deeper understanding takes time. Other times, meanings of things smack you with another Aha! experience.

The appearance of lights means you are transcending the mere physical state and entering the mental-spiritual super-sensory levels. To see the lights whether sitting or lying and with eyes closed, look upward between the brows.

The Moody Blues sang about breathing and lights in their magnificent rendition of *One Step Into the Light*, from their album, *Octave*, released in 1978. Some of the lyrics....

Above the dark despair
shines a light that we can share
Close your eyes and look up between your brows
Then slowly breathing in
feel the life force streaming in....

If you've never heard this sung by them, please find it online and listen. Not only do the words penetrate deeply into my mind, but the voices, diction and accompanying music fit. This is probably top of my list of all-time favorites of meditative music.

Lights, Colors and Phenomena

Exactly what happens during deep levels of meditation? It depends on which form of consciousness you pursue according to culture and teachings.

Some say the lights and colors represent various elements of our spiritual nature, our soul. Some teach that we shouldn't focus on the lights but simply let them pass. Though I have never tried to keep them with me through all these years, they have never left. The pros and cons of seeing or watching the lights in meditation are compelling, if not confusing. Others list colors and their meanings and what part of the spiritual body is represented. Further study provides each seeker with what is valid for him or her.

Light(s) appearing is a signal of transcending physical consciousness.

Once meditation is established, these lights come and go, sporadic in the beginning, bursting here and there before disappearing. They may seem to come from the forehead between the brows or from the top of your head. They may pulse toward you from out of nowhere or recede and fade.

The longer you meditate, and on a regular basis, the longer they remain. Any movement of the physical body during this part of meditation causes the lights to cease. Breathe slow and steady, although I have found my breath and heart rate speeding up for a particularly fantastic display.

With the onset, you may see swirling white light that, over time, stabilizes. Often times it's a combination of white with a yellow tinge.

Some Hindu teachings say that focusing straight into it helps it stabilize into an orb of pure white among the swirls. It takes a bit to accomplish this but may happen if you stay with your practice.

Along with this, my own visualizations contain something looking like mesh or the cross-weaving of netting, the threads formed of seemingly electrified blue-white lines. The fragment of mesh slips around within the area of my vision, sometimes pulsating in one area, then fades. Other times it spirals around the outer periphery of the blue/purple light. Sometimes I see what resembles a fingerprint swirling in a spiral effect

At first, it was dizzying but now I look forward to all of this. If my blue/purple light is not there soon as I close my eyes, it soon bursts forth, a circle, sometimes oval, sometimes emanating flowing electric hues and moving about. Often, it switches back and forth between indigo blue and glorious deep purple. The colors are said to signify changes taking place in consciousness.

Sometimes the blue/purple shows from a different perspective. The best I can describe it is as if looking straight down over a water drop that falls. When it lands, it splashes in droplets and blobs and streaks flying in all directions. Sometimes when it splashes it seems to fall all over me. Yet, in the middle of it all is that same blue/purple light giving off these magnificent emanations.

While this is happening, I know I am receiving from the Highest Source possible while in the physical body.

In meditation we cannot overlook or deny the effects of Indian teachings, which is where my search took me. It does not mean we must become the religion to make it work for us. Simply, the Hindus have been using these techniques for eons of time. Much of their knowledge helps any modern-day meditator cut through centuries of information to find what helps in these times.

The blue/purple emanation is what Swami Muktananda (1908 – 1982) termed the *Blue Pearl*. In his book, *Does Death Really Exist?* he says:

"The blue dot, which we call the Blue Pearl, dwells in the sahasrara, the spiritual center in the crown of the head. It is the body of the Self. All consciousness is contained in it. All of the dynamism of the breathing process comes from the Blue Pearl."

Muktananda added that the Blue Pearl is:

141

"...a physical manifestation of the soul. Seeing it in meditation is to see your soul."

We are the Light. It is that which gives life to the physical body through which we express ourselves.

A great many people now see the Blue Pearl during meditation because overall consciousness of humanity is elevating. It is said that for this to happen one needs to maintain the purest of thoughts and words. By meditating on the Blue Pearl with clear intent, we experience our true nature.

There is a dichotomy here however. While we strive to reach the highest levels of consciousness through meditation, we must also live and function in the world and society as we know it.

The purpose of meditation is to bring both into balance and become one true life.

More About Those Lights

The lights of my inner sight pulse, slip around in different directions, brighten and fade then brighten again, all uncontrollable on my part. They are simply there doing what they're meant to do. Sometimes I see sudden streaks of electric light flash toward the top of my head from the center of my Light Show.

In addition to the mesh pattern mentioned earlier, different textures appear off and on and I do not try to control them. I simply watch and try to contain my excitement. Often times I see flashes of stars, like fireworks. It truly is a Light Show. This has gone on most of my life time. Can you imagine why my mother never had trouble putting me to bed as a child?

According to some teachings, colors represent different levels of consciousness though accomplished teachers interpret various meanings. Sometimes you may see only yellow, or white or vague colors. Sometimes you see them all in one meditation sitting. Allow them to be and focus on them but simply watch. Allow what comes through to simply be. It is the help that your consciousness needs at that moment. Some of the interpretations of color phenomena include:

* Pure white, carrying an electric blue quality, is your higher consciousness at work.

* Yellow is believed to be symbolic of learning and/or teaching.

* Red signifies work in the physical or material realms.

* Blue/purple or the Blue Pearl, is your soul, and the highest level of consciousness while in the body.

These definitions vary from teacher to teacher. Some advise that we should stop watching the colors and bring attention back into our center in order to make spiritual progress. If you follow this school of thought, then seeing colors and lights represents a message to refocus attention and perception.

Other teachers say various colors are messages of healing going on in different parts of the ethereal body. They say to allow them to be but not concentrate on them.

As meditation deepens, when you feel that stirring of the mind, some people, like me, feel it in the brain itself, like a rocking back and forth movement or light-headedness. This is not the same light-headedness felt as if you're about to faint. It's the soul or ethereal body being stimulated. When this happens to me, though I may be lying flat on my bed, my head and sometimes my upper torso feels like I am nodding, though no part of my body is actually moving. Sometimes my entire body feels like floating, but I simply concentrate on my Light Show.

You may feel it kinesthetically through your entire body. You instantly realize how good this feels. Something is happening! Allow it to continue. Once you recognize this feeling, you'll hunger for it, so much so that there is no excuse, no thoughts of missing meditation. In your meditations, you begin to wait for this feeling, even expect it. Doing so deepens concentration and takes your attention to the center of your being. This feeling and all that comes with it is your direct link to higher consciousness where everything that is originates.

Be wary of any teachings that promise instant progress. Meditation is a practice that takes patience and commitment. Meditation is the ultimate way to pull your life together, release emotional blocks and bring in the good that is yours.

* * *

Shri Anandi Ma, an Indian holy woman, says that after reaching higher levels of meditation....

"...the benefits are intensified and encompass more subtle realms. The student can achieve peace and mental control, can become more creative, can develop a profound understanding of nature and experience inner joy. The aspirant becomes a stronger individual, a more complete person who can function in adverse circumstances with great poise, and is able to consciously absorb prana [energy and healing] from the universe and direct it for physical and mental well-being. Ultimately, the student encounters total reality, the absolute truth, knowledge of the Self."

Conclusion

Hypno-Scripts, and how you use them for either self-hypnosis or meditation, open the door to your true self.

The overall consciousness of human beings is evolving to a higher plane. Become a conscious part of it! It is the process of life, the reason for living.

While this book is meant to help open the window to self-hypnosis or meditation, the serious minded is encouraged to study all that can be accomplished as either or both of these modalities becomes a dedicated practice. The rewards are great and nearly indescribable.

People cannot be forced to do something their level of consciousness is not ready to experience. Some religions teach it is a sin to examine the mind or entertain the thought of higher consciousness in this lifetime. It is their prerogative to teach what they believe to those who would follow.

Non-believers teetering on the cusp of the possibilities may think teachings such as these to be a lot of unfounded New Age hocus-pocus. Yet, if they will but close their eyes they would soon see Truth.

Some may think these techniques wouldn't work for them. I advise to immediately stop and listen to that negative thought. Change from, "Well, this probably wouldn't work for me" into "I can make this work for me." Simple as that. Then begin to practice.

Use the scripts provided or write new ones for either meditation or hypnosis to effect positive change in your life. Read widely to increase your knowledge. Saturate your mind with what you wish to accomplish. Practice. Only you can make that happen.

Self-hypnosis is meant for enhancing your abilities and giving yourself suggestions for change. It opens the mind to super-consciousness. Whether you use only hypnosis or progress into meditation and deeper realms, hypnosis can remove blocks and give you access to abilities you may have only dreamed of accomplishing.

Meditation is for being still, not planning or dictating what is to come, but to receive from the Highest. Super-consciousness is endless. Why should your abilities be limited?

The state of consciousness that leads to the desire to know what's next appears when a person has turned the mind away from useless temptations that lead nowhere. Yet, it doesn't end there. Reorganization of our true selves and potential as a soul experiencing embodiment begins. It's a time when a person has risen above the travails of human life through a deeper state of mind.

As you practice self-hypnosis and/or meditation and realize the transparency that separates these two states of super-consciousness, you will have found the entry to your true self. You are unleashing the power of your mind. A new positive level of being that pales all other pursuits awaits your exploration.

The instructions in this book are not the final word on hypnosis or meditation. Nothing can be final because the human mind and spirit is infinite and forever evolving. These instructions are to further your knowledge in one obscure area to unleashing the power of your mind. Continue to read, study and learn about related topics of interest to round out your experience and enhance what you learn here. My hope is to provide incentive to others to begin this joyous journey.

SOME AFTER-THOUGHTS:

Much of the information in the meditation section of this book is for beginners or practitioners who would seek to learn more about meditation. Yet, I want to close leaving something special for the advanced student who, having already delved deeply into elevating consciousness, is familiar of the Kundalini life force.

The following are informative books for the true seeker as well as the sincere beginner.

Both of these books are out of print but used copies are still available on various websites. Simply do a search for the titles. I would advise securing a copy of the following all-inclusive texts before they are no longer available. I retain my copies because these two have eye opening information that answered many, many questions and validated what I experience.

Without alluding to any religion or specific version of the Book, for the advanced interested in learning about how Kundalini is cloaked in the Bible, I'd recommend *The Bible and Kundalini Energy*, by Dorothy Elder. The author discusses where the natural human abilities are cloaked in the wording of the Bible. This is a book for those who search diligently to learn about the energies of Illumination. From the back cover:

"Dorothy Elder's book, *The Bible and Kundalini Energy*, brings insights into the mystical consciousness of the Bible and breakthrough moments for those who are seeking integration of Eastern and Western spiritual paths." (Statement given by Marj Britt, Ed.D.)

* * *

Early in my life, I went through many stages and experienced much phenomena. The one book that explained almost all of it to my satisfaction was *Energies of Transformation: A Guide to the Kundalini Process*, by Bonnie Greenwell, PhD, Transpersonal Psychotherapist and Yoga teacher. I read this book almost before I knew what the term Kundalini meant. From the back cover:

"A synthesis of Eastern and Western perspectives of the ancient phenomena known as Kundalini awakening, including 23 fascinating case histories culled from the literature and recorded in interviews with Westerners who have lived through the process and found it to be a profound life-transforming experience that forever changed them physically, emotional and spiritually."

Contributors and Their Books

Randal Churchill is Founder and Director of the *Hypnotherapy Training Institute*, which draws many students each semester to San Francisco from around the world. He was the first President of the *American Council of Hypnotist Examiners*. He has taught at numerous institutions, including teaching psychiatrists at *Napa State Hospital*. He is the author of the award-winning classics *Regression Hypnotherapy* and *Become the Dream*, and the acclaimed *Catharsis in Regression Hypnotherapy*. Find his books here:

Amazon Author Page: http://tinyurl.com/peutk8x

Barnes & Noble: http://tinyurl.com/og37bpr

Books-A-Million: http://tinyurl.com/nuadf3j

Hypnotherapy Training Institute offers classes in California's Bay Area in Corte Madera. For more information:

http://www.hypnotherapy.com

Michael Angley, Colonel, *United States Air Force* (ret), Senior Supervisory Special Agent, *Air Force Office of Special Investigations* (ret)

His award-winning trilogy of books, *Child Finder*, *Child Finder: Resurrection* , and *Child Finder: Revelation* can be found at:

Amazon: http://tinyurl.com/n8k3sxs

Barnes & Noble: http://tinyurl.com/ocmvl4v

Books-A-Million: http://tinyurl.com/ohvn5xd

His website: www.mikeangley.com

Bibliography

Brennan, Barbara Ann (Reissue Edition 2011,March 23). *Hands of Light: A Guide to Healing Through the Human Energy Field*

Elder, Dorothy (1997, April). *The Bible and Kundalini Energy*

Greenwell, Bonnie, Ph.D. (2nd Edition 1995, February 1). *Energies of Transformation: A Guide to the Kundalini Process*

Kai, Joshua, ND *(2015, February 5).The Quantum Prayer: An Inspiring Guide to Love, Healing and Creating the Best Life Possible*

Swami Muktananda (1908–1982) (2nd Edition 1995, January 1).*Does Death Really Exist?*

Williamson, Marianne (2009, October 12). *A Return to Love: Reflections on the Principals of A Course in Miracles*

Author Biography

Mary Deal, a retired Clinical Hypnotherapist and lifelong practitioner of Self-Hypnosis and Meditation, has coached others in discovering their own creativity and establishing or deepening meditation practices. After a car accident ended her ability to maintain a hypnotherapy practice, a career change into creativity led to becoming an award-winning novelist and writer.

She has also published a short story collection and writers' references. She is a Pushcart Prize nominee, artist and photographer, and former newspaper columnist and magazine editor. A native of California's Sacramento River Delta, she writes from her home in Honolulu, Hawaii. You may contact her through the *Contact Me* page on her website *Write Any Genre*, listed in the Find Her Online section on the next page.

Find Her Online

Her Website: http://www.writeanygenre.com
Amazon Author Page: http://tinyurl.com/3z8pm31
Barnes & Noble: http://tinyurl.com/o7keqf7
Smashwords: http://tinyurl.com/6hagnv2
Linked In: http://www.linkedin.com/in/marydeal
FaceBook: http://www.facebook.com/mdeal
Twitter: http://twitter.com/Mary_Deal
Google+: http://tinyurl.com/pee51xz
Goodreads: https://www.goodreads.com/MaryDeal
Cold Coffee Cafe: http://coldcoffeecafe.com/profile/MaryDeal
BookTown: http://booktown.ning.com/profile/MaryDeal
Authorsdb: http://tinyurl.com/nnbk7lo

Her Art Galleries

Mary Deal Fine Art
    http://www.marydealfineart.com
Island Image Gallery
    http://www.islandimagegallery.com
Mary Deal Fine Art and Photography
    https://www.facebook.com/MDealArt
Pinterest
    https://www.pinterest.com/1deal